CONTENTS

MARCO ⊕ POLO
COSTA DEL SOL
GRANADA

There are five symbols to help you find your way around this guide:

★

Marco Polo's top recommendations – the best in each category

❂

sites with a scenic view

◉

places where the local people meet

♙

places where young people get together

(104/A1)
*pages and coordinates for the Road Atlas of the Costa del Sol
and the City Map of Málaga*
(U/A1) *coordinates for the City Map of Granada inside back cover*
(O) *area not covered by maps*
*For your orientation even places that are not marked in the
Road Atlas are provided with coordinates.*

*This travel guide was written by Roland Mischke.
As a journalist he travelled often through Andalusia
and wrote for German newspapers.*

MARCO ⊕ POLO

Travel guides and language guides in this series:

Alaska • Algarve • Amsterdam • Australia/Sydney • Bahamas • Barbados
Barcelona • Berlin • Brittany • Brussels • California • Canada • Channel Islands
Chicago and the Great Lakes • Copenhagen • Costa Brava/Barcelona
Costa del Sol/Granada • Crete • Cuba • Cyprus • Dominican Republic
Eastern Canada • Eastern USA • Egypt • Florence • Florida • French Riviera
Gran Canaria • Greek Islands/Aegean • Hong Kong • Ibiza/Formentera
Ireland • Israel • Istanbul • Italian Riviera • Jamaica • Lanzarote • London
Los Angeles • Madeira • Mallorca • Malta • Menorca • Mexico • Netherlands
New York • New Zealand • Normandy • Norway • Paris • Portugal • Prague
Rhodes • Rocky Mountains • Rome • San Francisco • Scotland • South
Africa • Southwestern USA • Switzerland • Tenerife • Thailand • Turkish
Coast • Tuscany • USA: New England • USA: Southern States • Venice
Washington D.C. • Western Canada • Western USA

French • German • Italian • Spanish

*Marco Polo would be very interested to hear your
comments and suggestions. Please write to:*

North America:
Marco Polo North America
70 Bloor Street East
Oshawa, Ontario, Canada
(B) 905-436-2525

United Kingdom:
GeoCenter International Ltd
The Viables Centre
Harrow Way
Basingstoke, Hants RG22 4BJ

*Our authors have done their research very carefully, but should any errors or omissions
have occurred, the publisher cannot be held responsible for any injury, damage
or inconvenience suffered due to incorrect information in this guide*

Cover photograph: Swimming bay Cala Honda in Nerja (Schapowalow: Thiele)
Photos: R. Irek (22, 36, 45); V. Janicke (28); G. Jung (16, 21, 64); K. Kallabis (12, 42, 77, 98);
Lade (92); Mauritius: Hubatka (103), Krautwurst (47), Thonig (49, 52, 58, 67);
M. Strobel (4, 6, 9, 26, 34, 60, 68, 89); P. Trummer (18, 24, 56)

2nd revised edition 2001
© Mair Geographischer Verlag, Ostfildern, Germany
Author: Sally Roy, Using Dupion
English edition 2001: Gaia Text, Munich
Editorial director: Ferdinand Ranft
Chief editor: Marion Zorn
Cartography for the Road Atlas: © Mairs Geographischer Verlag
Design and layout: Thienhaus/Wippermann
Printed in Germany

Discover Granada and the Costa del Sol!

Life is full of sensuous joy in this multicultural cradle of tolerance

When the evening settles over the gardens of Generalife, the Alhambra begins to shine like a jewel. The wind rustles in the oaks and cypresses, the water in the fountains burbles gently, shadows scurry across walls that with their engraved embellishments evoke memories of long-lost potentates. Within the old walls of the Alhambra, it seems as if time has melted and become petrified forever. The reddish walls of the Alcazaba, whose hue changes from hour to hour over the course of the day as they absorb the sunlight now begin to light up from within. You can still distinguish the neatly laid-out surrounding gardens with their roses, palm and laurel trees set against a background of magnificent mountains, the gates and patios, the eroded bricks of the protective walls, the almost exaggerated refinement of the ornamentation in the passages and chambers of the palaces. Then the night comes down like a black cloth and envelops this wonder.

The Alhambra sinks into solitude. By day you probably frequently find yourself lost in unbelieving astonishment as you wander around the palaces, the monuments of a lost orient, but now is the time when the imagination comes to life. In Italy the thing that travellers notice most is the art that they encounter in its excessive bounty at every step; here in Spain it is the legacies of the past that they find everywhere. Every tree, every stone, every twist of the road, every hill – history, history. "Give him alms, lady, for there is no greater loss than to be blind in Granada." This four-line-poem is mounted on ceramic on the wall surrounding the Alhambra. The city in the east of Andalusia, nestling on two ledges beneath the blue-green slopes of the Sierra Nevada, bor-

*As proud as a Spaniard.
Even a simplistic cliché
sometimes contains a grain of truth*

A masterful combination of arts near the Sierra Nevada: the Alhambra

dered to the west by a fertile, green belt of land, strikes visitors more than anything else as a jewel of architecture and a treasure trove of a great history. People first began to settle on its hills in the 5th century, but up until the 13th century, they remained dispersed. Neither the Romans, nor the Visigoths, nor any of the other nomadic nations felt the slightest inclination in this ancient melting pot of peoples to create urban settlements.

This changed with the rise of the Islamic Nasrite dynasty, founded in 1238, which resisted the permanent siege of the Christians right up until 1492 and in two and a half centuries nurtured a unique, never to be seen again, Islamic culture into full bloom on Spanish soil. This period also witnessed the construction of the Alhambra, the royal residence of the Moorish ruler of Granada, included by UNESCO on its World Heritage List. The troops of the Catholic monarchs Ferdinand and Isabella fought for ten years for the kingdom of Granada, until the last bastion of the children of Allah on the Iberian Peninsula was taken and the triumphal march of Islam in Europe was ended for good. The city was handed over without suffering any damage, after the wise Nasrite ruler Boabdil negotiated a treaty with the Spanish king in 1491–92 that granted safe conduct to the Moorish king following the surrender. So it was that the conquerors marched into an intact city, where the Arab influences of the past live on not only in the shape of Moorish historical buildings but also in the name of the city itself: Granada comes from the Moorish "Karnattah" and not from the Spanish word for pomegranate *(granada)*, a fruit which in fact features on the city coat of arms.

The most imposing works of architecture in Andalusia are of Moorish origin, the whole culture of the region is inspired by Arab influences. Many caliphs were highly educated and their love of rhetoric meant that scholars and authors gathered around them. The long period of Moorish rule was of benefit to the whole of Spain. Christians from other parts of the country sent their sons to study in the Arab south. Arts and sciences also flourished under the rule of the half moon. The way that Jews, Muslims and Christians lived here in close contact with one another in a spirit of tolerance was to be found nowhere else in Europe – until the Christian Reconquista replaced this unique culture with intolerance and religious fanaticism.

Under Moorish rule, the city had a multicultural population, where trends were set by Jewish doctors, diplomats and philosophers – to such a large extent that, at the time, Arab Granada was known as "the city of the Jews" – and its Islamic rulers were at pains to stay on good terms with the Christian Castilians. The city was planned and developed, irrigation systems were laid out; medicine, sculpture, art and poetry, song and dance were inspired by the extremely fruitful atmosphere of the epoch. The population grew to 200,000, four times that of contemporary London. The spirit of this "Golden Age" still lives on deep in the soul of Granada today. The honour-blood-race-nation ethos, this fascistoid ideological concoction that was widespread in Spain above all in the Franco era never fell on fertile soil here. The people of Granada of today remain, as ever, open minded, of liberal disposition with a predominantly youthful population. This young, innovative spirit lends even greater beauty to this venerable old city, and this is all the more reason to pity the blind man who is unable to behold this city in wonder and to tremble in delight at its architectural heritage. Change of scene: Feria in Torremolinos. This is where you can experience first hand the meaning of the expression "as proud as a Spaniard". Running straight through the middle of the gigantic, concrete mountains of what used to be a romantic fishing village before it soared up into the sky and stretched out to fill up all the available space, is the pedestrianised Calle San Miguel, one of the main arteries of the town, lined with splendid houses, restaurants and boutiques. First balcony doors open, then windows, and soon the pedestrianised zone is packed full of dancers. Young women in stunningly multicoloured, deep cut, frilled dresses; young men with tightly-fitting trousers and embroidered jackets down to the hips and flat hats. Whilst the women move graciously over the paving stones, the men put on airs. Happiness, *joie de vivre*, not least the escape from everyday cares, even a craving to be the centre of attention. The boots stamp, the castanets click, the dresses swing, the eyes shine. This is physical exercise with more than just a touch of eroticism. We are on the Costa del Sol, the coast that enjoys more sun than any other in Europe. *Joie de vivre* is a way a life here, and nobody is afraid to show it.

The concrete fetishists of the sixties and seventies didn't help much. Things were taken to extremes during the boom period, when package tourists came in swarms from Northern Europe to the sunny south, and swathes of coastline were covered in concrete. Places like Torremolinos and Fuengirola were crammed full of hotels that were nothing more than soulless boxes. From the sea off Torremolinos the holidaymaker could look out over the faded straw of thousands of parasols to survey an almost continuous ten-kilometre-long concrete wall stretching from the Playa del Saltillo in the west up to the Playa de los Álamos in the east. The sea was polluted, the beaches dirty, noise and smell made it impossible to get a bit of relaxation, and increasing crime was the last straw that left the image of the Costa del Sol at the absolute rock bottom. In the eighties, increasing numbers of environmentally-aware holidaymakers gave the coast the cold shoulder and in the eyes of the tourist industry, the Costa del Sol had gone out of fashion.

The concrete wall is still with us, but the high-rise blocks, apartment complexes and large hotels have now long since put the wild days of the founding of mass tourism behind them. Large-scale alterations and rebuilding have succeeded in giving the monotonous landscape a more human face – flowers bloom on the balconies, 15-floor façades are now covered in the rich green of plants. The connivances of politicians, get-rich-quick builders, finance and real estate sharks, tax-avoidance artists and land spectators have now been reined in, and the beaches have now become so clean that they win one EU award after another. Teams of cleaners swoop onto parks and promenades like commandos,

trees are planted in abundance. The tourist police in their snow-white uniforms or high up on horseback keep the peace. A cleverly conspired network of bypasses and highways has syphoned the worst of the traffic out of the towns that follow one another in close succession along the coast. Nature parks are being set up countrywide, 18 per cent of the 87,000 sq km area of Andalusia has been placed under some kind of protection.

It is still premature to report the death of the cliché of the kilometres of urbanizaciones, unimaginative holiday complexes and bungalows, but the open-minded traveller will be able, with a little effort, to find unspoiled corners and hidden little nooks and crannies even in a sea of stone houses like Torremolinos: terraces converted into gardens full of singing birds, balcony railings decked with tubs of flowers in alleys scarcely broader than your shoulders, street signs in the style of ornamental tiles on whitewashed walls, shady inner courts behind splendid wrought-iron railings, street processions smelling of fried food and laden with guitar music and heavy jasmine.

Off the former haunt of the well-to-do and aristocrats, Marbella, stylish, white yachts cruise once more. This architecturally bold agglomeration, set enchantingly against the mountainous landscape and the sea, blessed with the most pleasant of climates, was once known as the "Criminal Coast" owing to the fact that this was where film and television stars, the great names of music and influential people from the business world crossed paths with shady deal makers, oriental potentates, controversial political figures and the jet set. All of this has changed. Marbella has come down to earth, even if it still tends to put on airs with its architecture. The Andalusian hen on the Costa del Sol continues to lay golden eggs, but they no longer come out in quite as eccentric a shape as they used to in the past.

This is true of the whole coast. It no longer comes across as being stuck up and over done, instead it has taken on a new modesty. It no longer harbours pretensions towards being the playground for playboys and tarted-up stars past their sell-by date, but rather for guests who are hungry for the unaffected and the traditional – for this is an area where culture stretches back to the dawn of time. The first tourist on the southern coast of Spain was Old Stone Age man, who arrived about 22,000 years ago, and who was so satisfied that he never left. Cave graves, skeletons and holy places bear witness to a well-developed prehistoric culture. They were followed by Phoenicians, Greeks and Carthaginians, Romans, Visigoths and other peoples, each of whom left behind their own traces. Following the victory of the Christians over the Moors, who had stamped their mark on this region for almost 800 years (711–1492), Andalusia benefitted from Columbus's discovery of the New World and Spain's position as the most powerful nation in the world of the time. After this, the region sank into crippling poverty. It is one of the great paradoxes of history that Andalusia languished in obscurity for centuries, even

though it had once been the land of great dreams and events of genuinely earth-moving significance. The land that had served as the base for conquest of the New World declined into a backwater of peasants and day labourers, almost paralyzed by the heat and mesmerised by its own beauty, a place with a great past but no present.

It wasn't until the middle of the 20th century that Andalusia made contact with the modern world – thanks to tourism, which now brings more than six and a half million holidaymakers to its beaches each year. Now that this invasion has been survived, it is time for quality tourism, and this includes discovering the hinterland. In the mountainous region forming the backdrop to the

Sumptuous floral displays are to be found even in the narrowest of alleys

9

Costa del Sol, nature pulls out all the stops. You will find the flora and fauna of both Europe and Africa in this area, home to the Lynx, and where royal eagles brood, thousands upon thousands of migratory birds stop over, half-wild horses graze, and there are large numbers of storks and flamingoes. White villages are dotted like fields of snow over the hills of the Sierra. The visitor experiences a breathtaking variety of landscapes between sea level and the peaks at 3,400 m. Hairpin bends lead up wild, romantic mountains with stony crests, which look like oversized, bleached bones. Between red, naked cliffs lie dried-out river beds full of gravel. Fields of sunflowers covering hundreds of hectares turn into a yellow sea when they bloom, the olive plantations stretch as far as the horizon. The olive tree is the one permanent feature of this region. Even if all around there have been many changes, it remains untouched by the passage of time. It has been seen by every visitor since the Stone Age.

When it comes to romance, the inland has a trump or two up its sleeve against the coast. For example, its little squares overgrown with orange trees, its churches the size of cathedrals, so large that the posterity has considered their builders to be mad. The cool bodegas, where the fino matures in the sun in barrels decorated with coats of arms, its peace and quiet and scent of thyme and roses. Tiny villages perched like eyries on the sides of mountains. A church, the village square, surrounded by a scattering of whitewashed houses. Old women dressed in black, gnarled men, joyful children. Nobody in the whole of Catholic Spain is as God-fearing as the mountain people. Life means praying, baking sweet bread, marrying early, grafting away, keeping firm to the faith, and also celebrating with the same vigour. It is well worth stopping at random, strolling along the potholed roads and dropping in at the first bar you come to.

The landlord immediately polishes up the bar, then lays out little bowls with fleshy olives, a few calamares and manchego cheese dripping with oil, accompanied by honey-coloured wine from palomino grapes which leaves a taste of bitter almonds on the tongue. The television flickers away below the ceiling, the stone floor is covered in wood shavings, at the shabby tables sit simply dressed men, who first size up the newcomer out of the corner of their eye before they turn and smile shyly. You hear the same thing from foreigners who have spent time in the inland of Costa del Sol, mostly just a few kilometres away from the hustle and bustle of the coast: life here is so peaceful, so pleasant. The climate brings out a love of life in the people, it makes them relaxed, full of contemplation and inner peace. Taking things as they come has been made into an art here. These people, strongly connected to the earth, draw their strength from piety and *joie de vivre*, stern dignity and spontaneous joy. Visitors to the Costa del Sol today experience more than just the delights of a tourism infrastructure that aims for perfection – many pleasant, little surprises lurk in the most unexpected places.

History at a glance

Early history
Approximately 20,000 years ago Old Stone Age nomads settle on what today is the Costa del Sol

Around 1000 BC
Phoenician traders from the Eastern Mediterranean establish strongholds here

800–300 BC
First Greeks, then Carthaginians establish trading posts in South Spain

From 218 BC
Romans establish hegemony over the Iberian Peninsula

1 BC–3 AD
The peaceful conditions in the coastal region favour trade and prosperity

From 4 AD
Collapse of the Roman Empire. Power shifts from one Germanic tribe to another

711
The Arabs conquer Southern Spain and give it the name al-Andalus

8th–11th centuries
Economic and cultural blossoming under Islamic rule

Mid-11th century–15th century
Formation of small Islamic princedoms. Time and time again, Christian armies advance as far as Andalusia, which falls to Castile – right down to the kingdom of Granada

1492
The Nasrite kingdom of Granada surrenders to the Catholic monarchs Ferdinand and Isabella

From 1609
Expulsion of the Jews and the over 500,000 Muslims who had converted to Christianity

1704
Spanish War of Succession. The British occupy Gibraltar

End of 19th century
Economic decline resulting from the loss of the colonies

1931
Spain becomes a republic. The king leaves the country

1936–39
Following victory at the polls by the left popular front, General Franco stages a coup and crosses over with his troops from Spanish Morocco to Andalusia. The Spanish Civil War claims more than half a million lives

From 1960
The Costa del Sol becomes the tourist region of Southern Europe to attract the most visitors

1975
Death of Franco, King Juan Carlos becomes head of state

1981
Andalusia receives the status of "Autonomous Community"

1986
Spain enters the EC/EU

Bullfighters and demonic dancers

Where can you enjoy a heavenly stay? Who gets an ear as a prize? When are most Spaniards conceived?

Feria

Over the course of a year, more than three thousand festivals take place in the towns and villages of Andalusia: *ferias,* pilgrimages, carnivals, Islamic festivals and Christian processions. The term *feria* (correct translation: market, fair, although it covers a wide range of meanings) is used to describe the week of festivities in honour of the patron saint of a particular place. The true nature of the Andalusians comes out in their love of festivities: they immerse themselves fully in the whole affair and enjoy it all the more in the company of others. All festivities are occasions for expressing piousness and *joie de vivre*, pride and cheerfulness.

Flamenco

The Andalusian dance accompanied by song and the sound of the guitar derives from the *cante jondo,* the oldest form of song. The origins of the flamenco go back to Byzantine, Greek, and Arab times. It has many forms: alongside *sevillanas* and *fandangos,* in the

Joie de vivre in dance: the Flamenco

coastal region chiefly *granadinas* and *malagueñas* are performed – although not "real" flamencos in the strict sense of the word. The charm of the flamenco lies in its improvised rather than studied choreography. When the couple dancing manage to achieve a great level of intensity, Andalusian folk wisdom has it that the *duende* (demon) has entered them. The dance expresses the whole gamut of feelings ranging from zest for life to despair. For tourists, the most attractive things are the whirl of colourful skirts, the clicking of the castanets (which really have nothing to do with flamenco), the hand clapping and the stamping of the men's boots. The locals pay much more attention to the song, and in the case of the women dancers, the graceful movement of the arms.

Women

Little more than thirty years ago the feminine half of the Spanish world could do virtually nothing without the permission of fathers, husbands or priests: travel across the country required written permission, it was forbidden to open a bank account, frequently even going for a walk unaccompanied was frowned on, to say nothing of showing an interest in contraceptives and other such works of the devil. Whilst in the rest of Europe the movement for the emancipation of women marched on, in Spain patriarchy, church and poverty held women in subjugation. They suffered, above all in the middle and upper classes, under grotesque double standards according to which macho husbands were permitted to have mistresses, whilst at the same time erotic and sexual encounters by their wives were the object of revulsion. Premarital relations were also strictly ritualised, premarital sex was a sin, engagement a binding duty. This all changed radically after Franco – the explosive rage released by the desire to achieve emancipation overnight and a feminism that occasionally verged on militancy lead to uncertainty in the years following the death of the dictator. In the meantime, relations between the sexes have become less tense and radical feminism has died down. Even in the South of Spain most women now go out to work, marriage as an institution has lost its importance, the birth rate has fallen, there are more unmarried mothers and teenagers have access to contraceptives. Even so, a concept of masculinity and femininity has, particularly in Andalusia, lived on which emphasises the differences between the sexes, in which the women is sought-after and courted by the strong, protective man. The traveller time and time again encounters the clash between the modern and conservative image of women.

Lifestyle

"O Spaniard, who is capable of waking you from your deep slumber?" raged Casanova on his journeys in Spain. This question has not really turned out to be very prophetic. Following the sheltered era of protectionism under the dictator Franco, the Spaniards have set sail into the strong and often harsh wind of the free market – and are holding their course. The economic rise of Spain in the years of democracy has been significant and it has spawned a whole new generation of entrepreneurs and business people. Commerce and hard work, which at one time would have been beneath the dignity of a caballero, for whom idleness was a way of life if not a passion, are now seen as the prerequisites for success. In Andalusia, this has meant that many different customs and ways of life have become entangled with one another. For centuries there was virtually no change – now hardly anything is the way it used to be. The new approach to work demands new forms of behaviour. The Andalusians have become more open to the world, more tolerant, more flexible, more linguistically skilled. It is exciting to follow this process of social change, particularly for those who knew the Andalusia of old, where the clocks for so long ticked to a different rhythm. If there is one thing that the Andalusians have preserved, it is their way of not rushing headlong into a business deal. In Andalusia, directness rarely saves time. Even the toughest of negotiations are conducted in pleasant surroundings, for example over a meal lasting several courses and using carefully chosen colloquial forms of speech. "Genio y figura hasta la sepultura" – "Keep your composure and character, from the cradle to the grave!" No easy requirement, and one that still applies in the present day. It is not for nothing that this proverb still hangs on the walls of many Andalusian houses.

Paradores

They are expensive, but the experience is unforgettable. If you take an outside room on the top floor, you are nearer to the heavens than earth. From dizzy heights you enjoy a view down over the landscape with the silvery glimmer of its rivers, pale fields of wheat, and the panorama of the mountains. There is no more peaceful way to spend a night on the Costa del Sol. The *paradores*, of which there are no more than a dozen on the sun coast and the hinterland, are high-class hotels in former mansions, castles, stately homes, estates or monasteries, all restored in exemplary fashion. This splendidly up-market accommodation became available when the Spanish state bought up these empty historical buildings and took on responsibility for their upkeep, where others were unable to do so. By converting them into hotels, this architectural heritage has been preserved for posterity and at the same time these places of regional historical interest have been opened up to the public. Most of the *paradores* have spacious, comfortable rooms, a charming Andalusian patio, a courtyard with flowers, wrought iron and gurgling fountain, and frequently guests dine beneath the arch of a refectory at a table covered in damask set with

heavy silver cutlery. The *paradores* have their own unique atmosphere, which has been absorbed by their walls over the ages, and which sets them apart from modern hotels.

Religion

Spain is considered to be the most Catholic country in the world, and nowhere in Spain are the people more devoted to their religion than in Andalusia. But this is not an angst-ridden devotion fraught with seriousness, rather it is imbued much more with a worldly passion. A religious festival in the South of Spain without joy, dance and wine is scarcely imaginable. Even pilgrimages and processions, including those of the *Semana Santa,* the holy week preceding Easter, are not sorrowful affairs, but happenings to be experienced, where needless to say young people also participate. Religion in Andalusia is all about taking things easy. God and the saints may be exalted beings inspiring reverence, but at the same time they are regarded a little bit like good mates. In his book *The Spaniards and the Seven Deadly Sins*, Fernando Díaz Plaja imagines that his fellow countrymen have a private telephone line to God. They turn out to have no qualms about haggling with the supreme being: if a certain football team wins, alms will be given to the poor, if a business deal comes off, no adultery will be committed, if somebody's daughter passes an exam, the dog will never be kicked again. Such deals do not offend against the religious sentiments of the Andalusians. People here are totally natural in their dealings with the highest majesty. Despite this, they take their religion very seriously, and it is an indispensable part of their daily life.

Siesta

Many tourists make the mistake of underestimating the significance of this period of rest that occurs every afternoon – mainly between 3 pm and 5 pm. The siesta is the most noticeable feature of the rhythm of life in the south, which is hard for outsiders to comprehend. The main point, clearly, is to spend the hottest part of the day in a cool place. It is not, however, always the case that people use this time to rest: Spanish demographers have discovered that the majority of Spaniards are actually conceived during the siesta. After all, this period of rest is also the best possible preparation for the social life that fills the evenings and nights, and which the Andalusians love so much that they party their way right through to the early hours. You need to be in good condition to keep up with the pace, and the siesta is a great help in this respect.

Bullfights

The popular image of Spain is very much coloured by Andalusia, and above all because bullfighting has a special place in Andalusian folklore. The *aficionados,* as the fans are known, traditionally originate from here, as do the most famous bullfighters, who are called *matadores* in Andalusia. The Andalusians boast that they are the only ones to understand the true inner beauty of the *tauromaquia.* They allude here to the metaphysical dimension of the fight, where death is ever-present. The contest between man and beast within the framework of a strict set of rules corresponds to a need by the people to picture life and death as fate, complementing each other like two sides of the same coin. Animal rights activists who call for the abolition of bullfighting underestimate the serious ecological consequences this would have. "The fighting bull is related to the tame bull in the same way as the wolf to the dog", wrote Ernest Hemingway. The *toros bravos* are a separate breed of cattle, and would die out were it not for bullfighting. Until their death in the arena, they spend years grazing on land which also offers sanctuary to rare animals and plants. This would cease to be the case were it

The best view of the arena in Málaga is to be had from the mountain, Gibalfaro

not for these bulls, for the meadow land would be converted to intensive agricultural use. The economic influence of bullfighting and the *corrida* is also not be underestimated. It is the livelihood of thousands of Andalusians. The bullfights take place in the period between Easter and October, in many large towns every Sunday. This spectacle has of late enjoyed an unprecedented popularity. If in the past the *corrida* was considered to be a macho thing, nowadays more women than men attend the *fiesta nacional.* The spectators on the terraces are getting younger and younger. To get the most from bullfighting, you need to know some of the basic rules of the sport. After the *paseo,* the entry of the participants, three *matadores* (killers) make their entry, each of whom will fight two bulls. The *banderilleros* with their short, barbed spears and the mounted *picadores* with their lances, used to jab the bull in the neck muscles, do the bloody preparatory work and work the beasts up into a frenzy. In the *tercio de la muerte* (third of death) the *matador* comes on with the *muleta,* the red cloth. After he has tired the bull out with his adroit manoeuvres he attempts the *estocada,* the fatal sword blow. To do this, he endeavours with the aid of the *muleta* to lower the head of the bull, so that he can aim the fatal blow between the shoulder blades. If he has aimed correctly, he pushes the sword straight through to the aorta, causing the instant death of the massive beast. Should he miss, he risks courting the ridicule of the spectators and the animal is put out of its misery

with the *descabello,* the coup de grace. Depending on his performance, the *matador* is awarded by the *presidente* an ear, two ears or even the ears and tail of the bull. The latter is the highest accolade that may be bestowed in recognition of his art.

Beaches

La Marcha de Almería is a stretch of coast, palm-lined in places, stretching almost 50 km between Aguadulce and Adra. The *Playa de Velilla,* close to the town of Almuñécar, has up to now been spared from mass tourism. The area close to Nerja is characterised by its steep coastline interspersed with enchanting, little bays. The resorts of Málaga, Torremolinos and Fuengirola share 30 km of beach. Marbella's fine, sandy beaches are as chic as the town itself. Beaches of sand and dunes stretch all the way for 20 km from the Punta Mala as far as Gibraltar; all manner of flotsam is washed up here by the tide. At Tarifa the wind from the high dunes is blown into the eyes of walkers on the beach, and bare skin feels as though it is being pricked with pins. Even so, the stiff breeze is refreshing.

Water

Serious droughts in Andalusia are increasingly making the rationing of drinking water necessary. On the Costa del Sol water bans are introduced at times, and residents of Granada must also make do without water for several hours a day. Under the circumstances, you should do more than just show an understanding of the seriousness of the situation, and make an active contribution by using water sparingly.

In the home of tapas

Don't feast, have a nibble – but treat it as a ritual

Gazpacho was originally a dish for the poor, made from leftovers, but today it is on the menu at the most select restaurants. The most tempting delicacies are tiny, not enough to fill you, nothing more than a taster preceding the appetiser. What is to be made of the paradoxes of Andalusian cuisine? Learn to love it – for cooking, boiling, simmering and roasting is a labour of love here – an unusual mixture.

The inhabitants of the province of Granada and the Costa del Sol are died-in-the-wool Andalusians when it comes to food. For Basques and Catalans, the taking of food is a serious and drawn-out affair. For the Andalusians, it is a game. Galicians and people in Madrid take eating so seriously that the whole thing turns into a wearisome celebration. Not Andalusians; they don't want a feast, they want to have a nibble. Their idea of good food is something small, but tasty. A table

groaning with haute cuisine does nothing for them, but the thought of a *tapear* is enough to get them licking their lips. Tapas are to be found all over Spain, but have their origins in Andalusia and this is where they have been turned into a fine art.

Tapas are little morsels, one or two mouthfuls taken between drinks. Literally translated *tapa* means "lid". In the past, a glass of wine was served together with a little titbit that was intended to help it go down better: a piece of cheese, little bowl of olives, a slice of sausage or ham. Out of this custom, a whole new culinary culture developed. Andalusians love nothing more than wandering in small groups from pub to pub, where they have a beer or a glass of wine, accompanied by a tapas or two. There is no end to the variety – the landlord is free to use his imagination. There are anchovies marinated in vinegar with garlic *(boquerones)*, fried anchovies *(boquerones fritos)*, mushrooms with garlic *(champiñones al ajillo)*, stuffed mushrooms, the stuffing a closely-guarded secret of the landlord *(champiñones rellenos)*, prawns in garlic *(gambas al*

A heaven full of ham: the village of Trevélez in the Alpujarras is the ham capital of Spain

ajillo), skewered dates, wrapped in crisply fried bacon *(pinchitos con dátiles y bacon),* skewered pieces of marinated meat *(pinchitos morunos),* little tuna fish and olive pies *(empanadillas de atún y aceitunas)* or little fish balls in a piquantly spiced sauce *(albóndigas en salsa).*

One great thing is that you don't need to know any Spanish to order these delights that can stand in for a main meal. The various tapas are displayed behind glass under the bar, rather like visiting cards of the landlord, so that all you need to do is point to one and try it. And if you are really hungry, ask for a *ración:* this is a portion large enough to fill a small plate. Some visitors are said to have become so enchanted by the delights of the *tapear* that many months passed before they could find the slightest inclination to sit once more in a restaurant hacking away at a piece of meat. Tapas eating involves an element of surprise – you have to be prepared to encounter new tastes, to learn to activate your senses in new ways.

Gazpacho is made from anything that is left over and are based on a simple recipe. Ripe, juicy tomatoes, a cucumber, a pepper, onions, soaked stale bread, vinegar, olive oil, garlic – in the past, crumbs from the master's table, today a dish that has found recognition worldwide in gourmet establishments. The ingredients are pureed, salt and pepper are added, then the mixture is diluted with water. Then the soup needs to stay in the fridge for an hour or two. Anyone who has tried it comes to the conclusion that being a vegetarian is not as bad as they had previously imagined – as long as there is gazpacho.

Andalusian cuisine is anything but over the top. Compared to the other Spanish provinces, the emphasis here is on understatement. Whilst Galicia, Catalonia and above the Basque country have produced famous cooks, Andalusia is the *zona de los fritos,* the fried food zone. These dishes are not greasy, but rather lightly baked. The basic ingredient is above all fish and seafood. This is not to say that meat has no part to play, but the Andalusians are not as obsessed with it as other nations. This was enough to dismay Ernest Hemingway, who found that: "The Andalusians breed fine bulls, stage splendid fights with them and end their lives in a breathtaking manner – but they have no idea how to cook them". There is one exception here: the *rabo de toro,* braised oxtail, found frequently on the menu particularly in Granada. There is another meat speciality in the hinterland of the Costa del Sol, *jamón serrano,* ham from pigs which run free in huge oak forests, which is first salted in the snow of the Sierra and then dried in the mountain air. There doesn't exist a single Andalusian who can resist it.

The neighbours on the coast are experts in the art of preparing seafood. *Sopa de pescado,* a thick fish soup, and *pescado frito,* baked fish, are dishes which nobody else can make in quite the same way. The fish is so white and tender that you can scarcely believe that is has come into contact with oil. The use of spices is another art which has been perfected here. The Andalusian tortilla looks just like a flan and contains every kind of vegetable produced by the garden – but it is the spices that give it such an outrageously wonderful taste.

The simplest things are the best that the local cuisine has to offer. Baguette bread is sliced longways, the inside is spread with olive oil and filled generously with vegetables. A pinch of salt and pepper on top, a little oil is poured on, then all that is needed is a glass of red wine – it tastes so good that you go weak at the knees. Refreshing, spicy, crusty, crisp – just the job when you're in the gleaming Andalusian sun.

What is true for the whole of Spain is especially so in Andalusia in the hot South: in contrast to colder climes, meals are taken much later: lunch isn't until two or three o'clock and you have to wait until nine or ten pm for dinner, except in restaurants catering specifically for the tourist trade. When you are trying to track down the right restaurant, it pays to play it by ear. Let yourself be won over by the ambience and taken in by the atmosphere of a place. Don't commit yourself straight away by ordering a complete meal, instead start with a small sample, in other words try a few tapas. If they don't appeal to you, leave after ten minutes and head for the next restaurant. This is the way Andalusians go about it.

In terms of reputation, Andalusian wine is outclassed by sherry: the dry *fino* (it should be the colour of straw and well cooled) or the slightly nutty *amontillado* (a half-dry sherry), the dark gold *oloroso* or the sweeter, more appetizing *cream*, almost entirely destined for export. The Andalusians know best which wine should be enjoyed at which time of day. If you make the effort to observe and speak to them, you will see that the art of eating and drinking is simple. A lesson worth learning.

Whether a dry fino or a nutty amontillado: tapas are a must

From kitsch to genuine handicrafts

Caution is the order of the day in souvenir land

The most interesting is to be found in *Granada* – it has a tradition in Andalusia that stretches back over centuries; many techniques and patterns still in current use can be traced back to Moorish times. Ceramics in the form of pots and dishes are mostly original, always brightly coloured and almost always good value. You can tell Grenadine amphoras and water jugs from their distinctive green-blue pattern and the symbol of the pomegranate. It is also worth buying pottery from the village of *Coín.* The pretty tiles can really grow on you. You can easily buy them from sellers at the edge of the road. A tile in your bookcase or on your table will remind you of those happy days on the Mediterranean coast every time you see it. A souvenir that is both unusual and practical is a basket made of esparto grass, to be found in the villages of the *Alpujarras,* in *Antequera,* and also

on the coast. They are strong and mostly well shaped. In the inland towns and villages you should also keep your eyes open for wrought iron and silver filigree work, and also leather goods. These are often still genuine hand-made articles, fruits of traditional processes that soulless industrial products can never hope to match. Attractive embroidery is on offer in *Mijas,* some examples are the last word in kitsch.

If you see the sign "artespaña" hanging above the door of a shop, you know you can trust it. These state-supported enterprises are totally dedicated to preserving traditional handicrafts and absolutely none of the goods sold in them are made in Taiwan. Elsewhere you need to keep your wits about you. The Costa del Sol is souvenir land, and caution is the order of the day. Much of what is done in the name of commerce is little more than daylight robbery. Unfortunately, as long as there are gullible tourists, there will always be traders peddling junk.

Alcaicería in Granada:
Shopping in a bazaar atmosphere

Pilgrimages and water processions

*They know how to have a good time in Andalusia –
at equestrian events, bullfights and horse fairs*

When it comes to festivities, the Andalusians are champions. Not a day passes without the occurrence of a festival somewhere in the province of Granada and on the Costa del Sol. The most spirited celebrations usually take place in the villages, where things are still done in the good old-fashioned way: anarchistic, sensuous, powerful and mystical. And from time to time also deeply heathen, with rites that are older than the Christian faith that in places have been preserved intact. The priest prefers to turn a blind eye to them. The calendar of festivals in Andalusia is dictated by religious and worldly dates in equal measure. The fiestas in the South of Spain are particularly colourful and expressive. For information about the current calendar of festivals and for more detailed information, consult the tourist information offices.

Even the most hardened agnostic finds it difficult to resist the unique charms of the processions during the Semana Santa. The most impressive processions are to be seen in Málaga and in Granada

PUBLIC HOLIDAYS

If a public holiday falls on a Sunday, then the following Monday is a holiday. 1st January *(Año Nuevo)*, 6th January *(Epifanía)*, 28th February *(Día de Andalucía)*, Maundy Thursday *(Jueves Santo)*, Good Friday *(Viernes Santo)*, 1st May *(Fiesta del Trabajo)*, 15th August *(Asunción de Nuestra Señora)*, 12th October *(Día de la Hispanidad)*, 1st November *(Todos los Santos)*, 6th December *(Día de la Constitución)*, 8th December *(Día de la Inmaculada Concepción)*, 25th December *(Navidad)*

LOCAL FESTIVALS & EVENTS

January
On the 2nd, the *Día de la Toma* is celebrated in Granada, to mark the entry into the town of the *Reyes Católicos*.

The first Sunday sees the pilgrimage season begin in Almería with *Romería de la Virgen del Mar*.

On the 5th there is a huge equestrian procession in Málaga (*Cabalgata de los Reyes Magos*).

February
On the first Sunday, the faithful of Granada make the pilgrimage

to the Sacromonte in honour of the patron saint of the town, *San Cecilio*, accompanied by the guitar music of the gypsies – half of the town is on the move.

Carnival organisations ring in the *Carnival* in Málaga with processions.

March/April

To celebrate *Semana Santa,* Holy Week, the most spectacular religious festivals of the year take place everywhere. In the ★ *procession* in Málaga 35 guilds haul more than 70 monumental figures through the town. The Easter processions in Granada are well worth seeing.

May

At the beginning of the month, in many Andalusian towns the flower-decked *May crosses,* the *cruces de mayo,* are displayed.

June

The *Feria de San Bernabé* passes off in Marbella at the beginning of June with equestrian events.

June/July

At the end of June and the beginning of July, the ★ *Festival de Música y Danza de Granada (Tel. 0034/958 22 18 44; Fax 958 22 06 91; www. granadafestival.org)* takes place in Granada, an international festival of music and dance with world-famous soloists and ensembles.

July

At the beginning of July the *Feria y Fiesta Mayor* is held in Estepona: equestrian processions and contests in Andalusian costumes.

In mid-July the spectacle of *Virgen del Carmen* takes place in Fuengirola, a procession on the sea.

Colourful costumes are almost always part of the fiesta, frequently also horses

MARCO POLO SELECTION: FESTIVALS

1 Festival de Música y Danza in Granada
A particularly attractive festival with famous musicians and dancers (page 26)

2 Easter procession in Málaga
The Semana Santa in the principal city of the sun coast is the finest religious festival of the Christian West (page 26)

On the 25th July, not only in Galician Santiago, but also in the whole country, the day of the patron saint of Spain, *Santiago Apóstol,* is celebrated.

August

In the middle of the month, the *Feria de Málaga* is held in the town centre and on the Málaga trade fair site. It lasts for a week, there are daily bullfights, colourful tents are pitched on the park promenades, and the celebrations go on until late in the night.

Mid-August also sees the *Fiestas de la Recolección* in Antequera: bullfights, street shows, a variety of sporting contests, accompanied by a large cattle market.

Also in the middle of the month there is the *Fiesta de la Virgen de la Antigua* in Almuñécar; nightly water processions are organised in honour of the patron saint of the town.

The *Feria de San Roque* in Torrox bei Nerja, famous for its Fireworks, also takes palce in the middle of August.

In the middle of the month, a *Flamencofestival* is held in Benalmádena to honour Nuestra Señora de la Cruz.

The last week sees the *Feria* in Almería, where an international music festival also takes place.

September

It is a delight to watch the contestants decked out in splendidly colourful costumes for the flamenco and dancing competitions at the *Fiesta de la Virgen de la Peña* in Mijas, which takes place in the first half of the month. At the *Encierro Taurino* as part of the feria of Mijas, young bulls are driven through the streets.

The *Día del Turista* is celebrated in Torremolinos on the first Thursday of the month, with ostentatious shows and cultural offerings.

Towards the end of the month, the *Feria de San Miguel* is celebrated in Vélez-Málaga. As well as a cattle market and a fair, there are also flamenco contests.

October

On the first Sunday and the following three days, there are folklore performances as part of the *Feria* in Fuengirola.

November

International *jazz festival* in Almería.

December

On one Sunday, the traditional pig-slaughtering festival *La Matanza* takes place in Pampaneira. Lively atmosphere. For the most part, the blood of fattened piglets flows.

Arabia in Europe

*Wild mountain heights, cave dwellings
and a veritable wonder of the world*

At the foot of bald-headed, hunch-backed mountains, tucked in between the slopes, the villages shimmer in the hazy light. The road leading up to them can scarcely be described as asphalted, so numerous are the potholes, and it gradually turns into a gravel track. It runs across hilly

*A garden of Eden, a cool,
green paradise: the Generalife
helps you to forget all about the heat,
noise and dust of the city*

terrain, past fincas and olive groves, becoming bumpier all the time, with ruts and furrows and stones the size of a head. The road is now nothing more than a mountain track, no more crash barriers to interrupt the view of the imposing, rocky backdrop, the rough beauty of the boulders and shattered rock faces, into which the forces of weathering gnaw incessantly. This territory is for mules, not for tyres. The Sierra Nevada is a wild and precipitous part of the world. Water

Hotel and restaurant prices

Hotels
Category 1: from 15,000 Ptas
Category 2: 10,000–15,000 Ptas
Category 3: up to 10,000 Ptas

Restaurants
Category 1: from 7,000 Ptas
Category 2: 4,000–7,000 Ptas
Category 3: up to 4,000 Ptas

The prices are for a double room with breakfast. If there is no breakfast, join the Andalusians in the bar!

The prices are for a typical meal (generally three courses) with half a litre of wine per person.

Important abbreviations

Av.	Avenida (Avenue)	**Pl.**	Plaza (Square)
Ctra.	Carretera (Country Road)	**s/n**	sin número (no number)
C.	Calle (Street, Road)	**Urb.**	Urbanización (Settlement)

MARCO POLO SELECTION: GRANADA AND THE SIERRA NEVADA

1 Albaicín
Picturesque former Moorish-quarter for romantic evenings and view of the Alhambra and Sierra Nevada (page 31)

2 San Jerónimo
Secluded inner courtyard of a monastery where the past comes to life (page 38)

3 Patio de la Acequia im Generalife
Square with water jets and lots of plants. A place for meditation and silent contemplation (page 35)

4 Las Alpujarras
Wild mountainous landscape on the southern slopes of the Sierra Nevada with hidden villages (page 48)

from melting snow has eroded through gneiss and slate to leave deep gorges. It is nothing short of a miracle that people live here at all, when you consider that the barren soil from which they wrest their harvests lies mostly on steep slopes, and consists of scraps of land terraced into small strips rarely more than two or three hectares in size. The terraces, thanks to which the farmers are able to eke out a living, are the invention of the Arabs. More than 600 years ago, the Moors demonstrated how the art of irrigation could bring fertility to a barren region. Even though they have long since been banished, tradition still bears witness to the time when they shaped the destiny of this area.

Nowhere more so than in Granada (pop. 285,000), the urban centre at the foot of the Sierra Nevada. First referred to as Elibyrge in 5 BC and known as Iliberis in Roman times, it was the Moors that brought prosperity to this city. This point is brought forcibly home when you contemplate the Alhambra, a complex of fortresses, gardens and palaces from the 13th and 14th centuries, a relic of the Nazarie dynasty, and a kind of eighth wonder of the world. The whole city with its steep, narrow lanes running around the Alahambra, is a jewel of universal architecture. Many consider it to be the most beautiful city in all of Spain.

GRANADA

☛ City Map inside back cover

(107/E3) Sunday morning in the Plaza Nueva. Elderly women, some of them accompanied by their daughters, shuffle along on their way to the cathedral. Elderly men, some of them accompanied by their sons, stand and bluster in the rectangular, gently sloping square. Tourists get in supplies of reading material in their own language from the news stand. A young man with a thick mane of hair and a dishevelled, bushy beard has set up his stool in front of a restaurant and got his guitar out of its case. He carefully tunes the instrument on which he will play classical pieces right through to the evening, for which he is sure to be rewarded with a rich bounty of pesetas. A herd of joggers trot by. Cars struggle along the narrow lane leading past the church up to the Sacromonte. The hawk-eyed waiters have long since got their chairs and tables ready on the square and now stand in a state of readiness until some passersby metamorphose into voyeurs for the time it takes to drink a coffee. For is there a better reason to sit in this square than to watch? The Plaza Nueva was built as a meeting place. It is one of the most attractive squares in Spain and provides every visitor with an almost intimate window on the daily life of Granada.

SIGHTS

Albaicín (U/D-E2-3)

★ ⋙ Arabia in Europe: The narrow alleys and squares the size of a handkerchief to the north west of the Alhambra are the equivalent of the grid of an Arabian medina. The archtectural style of this quarter perched on a foothill of the Sierra de la Yedra also has an oriental flavour, where flower pots adorn the *carmenes,* as the country-style houses in the middle of the city are called, as do geometrical tile patterns, stucco ornamentation and pointed arches – particularly in the *Calle de Pagues (Casa de los Mascarones)* and in the *Calle de Pardo (Casa Morisca);* tiny vegetable gardens, alleys of staircases where washing hangs out and parts of the Moorish city walls. Granada's oldest quarter is a

maze where there are neither signposts nor main roads – you simply have to follow your nose. 12,000 people live here, and in the 1960s there were three times this number. In 1994, the Albaicín was declared a World Heritage Site by UNESCO. The central and most lively square is the *Plaza Larga.* In the white side streets of the Calle del Agua, a village-like peace and quiet hangs over the Albaicín, so close to, yet a million miles removed from, the city below where you can scarcely hear yourself think for the roar of traffic. Almost all of the nearly three thousand houses have fallen into a poetic state of decay. Those who experience the sunset from here, with the Alhambra set against the backdrop of the Sierra Nevada, will enjoy a "sight, which people from the north could not even begin to imagine" (Théophile Gautier). The best place to experience this intoxication of the senses is from the ⋙ *observation terrace* of the San Nicolás church. The Albacín is not a dangerous place – but it is best to err on the side of caution when you stroll through its alleys.

Alhambra (U/D-E3-4)

The facades are veritable Gobelins in stone. On the walls dance flowers, leaves, stars – and between them, the name of Allah, thousands of times, in white marble. Palaces are engraved as if they were pieces of jewellry. The whole Alhambra is a work of embroidery fashioned in stone. And in all manner of plants, with hedges serving as frames. Paths, flower beds and fountains are bordered by green strips of laurel, jasmine and orange trees. Arborvitae are trimmed into the shape of Arabian arched gateways and every rose bush is so carefully trimmed that you would think that all the gardeners here are required to undergo training in hairdressing.

With more than two million visitors annually, the best-preserved fortress of Islamic Spain is the most popular site with visitors. Its walls, crowned by green bushes against the background of the mostly snow-covered Sierra Nevada, are made of clay bricks containing iron which seem to glow red in the evening light. For this reason the Arabs called it *al hamra,* the red. The Christian conquerors superimposed a Renaissance palace on the oriental complex, thus imposing a forced union of this filigree work of Islamic architecture with a proud achievement of the Renaissance.

The *Alcazaba* fortifications are the oldest part, and were built even earlier than the Nasrite era in the 9th century. Its ✷ *Torre de la Vela* watchtower (No. 57 on the map) is 26 m high and offers a fine view of the Sierra Nevada. However, the ✷ square between Alcazaba and the Nasrite Palace affords the best view of Granada, especially of the Albaicín and Sacromonte quarters of the city. The *Mexuar,* the former audience and court chamber (13), was extended by the addition of a chapel in Christian times. In the neighbouring *Patio de los Arrayanes* (14), the myrtle court, visitors are enraptured by the long goldfish pond flanked by low hedges of myrtle and bordered at the narrow end by delicate arches. From here, dignitaries and ambassadors were led into the *Salón de Embajadores*

(15) the salon of ambassadors. This chamber on the ground floor of the *Torre de Comares* (16) was the centre of power in the palace. The domed ceiling of the almost 20-m-high chamber was made of cedar wood and inlaid with mother of pearl. The centre niche, opposite the door, was the site of the Sultan's throne.

The *Court of the Lions* (20) was part of the Sultan's private quarters. This is the very artistic heart of the Alhambra, through which – just like the four rivers of the Islamic paradise – water flowed from all four points of the compass along canals in the middle. The twelve lions, symbolising the eternal waters of paradise, spew out the collected water, are made of marble. Some 124 slender marble columns combine to form an ornate archway. The countless chambers round about the Court of the Lions exhibit a timeless elegance and are decorated using a stylised script. Each of these chambers, from which water flows to the lion fountains, has its own history. In the *Sala de los Abencerrajes* (21) on the south side, the Sultan had 36 noblemen from the Abencerrajes clan beheaded at the end of a feast under these splendid stalactite vaults. Opposite, the *Sala de las Dos Hermanas* (19), to the side of the court of lions, was where the Sultan's wife ruled the roost. One of the upper friezes is decorated with Arabic calligraphy, whilst the honeycomb ceiling is made of stalactites. Most of the private rooms grouped around the hall were reserved for the ladies of the harem, where they acted out their romances and wove their intrigues. With the exception of the concu-

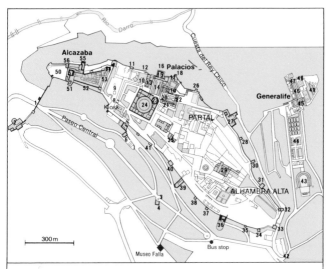

Alhambra and Generalife

1 Puerta de las Granadas
 (Gate of the Pomegranates)
2 Torres Bermejas
 (Red Towers)
3 Fuente del Tomate
 (Fountain of the Tomato)
4 Monumento a Ganivet
 (Monument to the
 Grenadine author)
5 Fuente del Pimiento
 (Fountain of the Pepper)
6 Pilar de Carlos V
 (Column of Charles V)
7 Puerta de la Justicia
 (Gate of Justice)
8 Puerto del Vino
 (Wine Gate)
9 Plaza de los Aljibes
 (Square of Wells)
10 Patio de Machuca
11 Torre de las Gallinas
 (Tower of the Hens)
12 Torre de los Puñales
 (Tower of the Dagger)
13 Mexuar
 (Former audience chamber)
14 Patio de los Arrayanes
 (Court of Myrtles)
15 Salón de Embajadores
 (Salon of Ambassadors)
16 Torre de Comares
17 Habitaciones de Carlos V
 (Chambers of Charles V)
18 Tocador de la Reina
 (Queen's Boudoir)

19 Sala de las Dos Hermanas
 (Salon of the Two Sisters)
20 Patio de los Leones
 (Court of the Lions)
21 Sala de los Abencerrajes
 (Salon of the Abencerrajes)
22 Sala de los Reyes
 (Salon of the Kings)
23 Krypta
24 Palacio de Carlos V
 (Palace of Charles V)
25 Baños (Baths)
26 Torre de las Damas
27 Torre de los Picos
 (Tower of the Battlements)
28 Torre del Cadí
29 Parador de San Francisco
30 Torre de la Cautiva
 (Tower of the Prisoner)
31 Torre de las Infantas
 (Tower of the Princesses)
32 Torre del Cabo de la
 Carrera (Tower at the end
 of the Race Track)
33 Torre del Agua
 (Water Tower)
34 Torre de Juan de Arce
35 Torre de Baltasar de la Cruz
36 Torre de Siete Suelos
 (Tower of the
 Seven Floors)
37 Torre del Capitán
 (Tower of the Captain)
38 Torre de las Brujas
 (Tower of the Witches)

39 Torre de las Cabezas
 (Tower of the Heads)
40 Torre de Abencerrajes
 (Tower of the Abencerranjes)
41 Puerta de los Carros
 (Tower of the Carts)
42 Eingang zum Generalife
43 Theater (Theatre)
44 Jardines nuevos
 (New Garden)
45 Pabellón Sur
 (South Pavilion)
46 Patio de la Acequia
 (Court of Streams)
47 Pabellón Norte
 (North Pavilion)
48 Patio de la Sultana
 (Court of the Sultana)
49 Jardines altos
 (Upper Garden)
50 Baluarte (Outwork)
51 Torre de la Pólvora
 (Powder Tower)
52 Jardines de los Adarves
 (Battlement Garden)
53 Torre Quebrada
 (Broken Tower)
54 Torre del Homenaje
 (Tower of Homage)
55 Torre de las Armas
 (Weapon Tower)
56 Torre de los Hidalgos
 (Tower of the Nobility)
57 Torre de la Vela
 (Watchtower)

Perfect symmetry and filigree marble: the Court of the Lions in the Alhambra

bines and their children, no mortal – servants didn't count – was permitted to set foot in this private section. The royal bedchamber *Sala de los Reyes* (22) is at the end of the Court of the Lions. One curious feature here is the court and hunting scenes painted on leather, even though pictorial representation was forbidden under Islam.

On the other side of the Lindaraja garden you come to the *Baños Árabes* (25), the Arab baths. Not far from the *Torre de las Damas*

(26), a princely country house with a gate of five arches beside a pond lined with laurel, oleander and palm trees is the terrace garden *Jardines del Partal,* a place imbued with harmony and beauty. After the gardens, don't miss the opportunity to take a walk along the towers that once protected the eastern part of the Alhambra.

Work on the massive *Renaissance palace of Charles V* (24), set on a square base, was started in 1526 following plans by Pedro Machucas, but it remained uncompleted even after 42 years of building work. Only the circular inner court surrounded by a gallery of columns around both of the two floors, which now house the *Museo de Bellas Artes (Mon–Sat 10 am–2 pm)* and the *Museo de Arte Hispano-Musulmán (Mon–Sat 10 am –2 pm)* was completed. The first of these is devoted especially to the works of Granadino artists, the second, capitals, clay and ceramic works. As a result of painstaking restoration work, the palace was returned to pristine condition and reopened in 1995.

If you get here too late (and that may mean after 10 am), don't be surprised if you are refused tickets. This is because only a limited number of visitors are allowed to enter everyday. It makes sense to reserve tickets in advance for a specific time (reservations are accepted for any time up to a year in advance) *(Tel. 902 22 44 60; Fax 958 21 05 84; from abroad Tel. 0034/13 74 54 20).* Payment is made by giving a credit card number or crediting the given account number. You then pick up your tickets and receipts 30 minutes before the appointed time of your visit. Advance tickets are also available locally at *Banco Bilbao Vizcaya. (Pl. Isabel la Católica; http://decompras.bbv.es). Mar–Oct. daily 8.30 am–8 pm, Tue–Sat also 10 pm–11.30 pm, Nov–Feb: daily 8.30 am–6 pm, Fri/Sat also 8 pm– 9.30 pm, nightly visits to the Nazarie palaces only, 1000 Ptas (including Generalife), reduced price 600 Ptas; www.alhambra-patronato.es*

Baños Árabes   (U/D3)

These baths dating back to the Arabs are even older than those in the Alhambra: the washing,

bathing and rest rooms were built as long ago as the 11th century, and attest to the importance attached by the Moors to personal hygiene and cleaning as a ritual. *Tue–Sat, 10 am–2 pm; entry free; Carrera del Darro 31*

Generalife   (U/F3)

Legend has it that the gardens on the hill opposite the Alhambra came into being for pedagogical reasons. The garden was laid out in the 14th century under the instructions of the worried Sultan, who was alarmed when astrologers prophesised that a great future awaited his son, provided he was first able to survive certain amorous adventures unharmed. To prevent this, the father decreed that the growing boy should be confined to a luxurious isolation. The boy was to remain undisturbed in a refuge full of jasmine, roses, oranges and myrtles where he would not have the slightest chance of making the acquaintance of the opposite sex and all the confusing feelings that this would engender.

The spacious garden is a masterpiece of landscape architecture. Its ⚜ main promenade affords a unique view of the Alhambra complex situated slightly below. The cypress allée leads past walls and towers to the old Franciscan monastery and the little Moorish palace behind which the maze-like gardens extend.

A particularly snug place is the ★ *Patio de la Acequia* (Court of the Stream, 46 on the map) with its water jets and rich variety of plants. Further uphill you come to the *Patio de los Cipreses* (Cypress Court) and the *Escalera del Agua* (Water Terraces), where wonder-

A bed made of Carrara marble: the monuments to Isabel and Fernando

fully cool water spills down in a series of terraces. In 1954, an open-air stage in the form of an amphitheatre (No. 43) was built and in summer this is the venue for the music and dance festival. *Opening times the same as for the Alhambra, combined ticket 1000 Ptas, reduced price 600 Ptas*

Cathedral Santa María de la Encarnación/Capilla Real (U/C3)

A huge, elaborate, spacious stone building from the 16th century. As one of the great churches of Andalusia, it is considered to be one of the finest sacred buildings of the Spanish Renaissance. The architect, sculptor and painter Alonso Cano (1601–1667), the greatest masterbuilder of the Granadino school, contributed to the construction work, which lasted almost 200 years. He was responsible for building the *Western Façade* with the three monumental arches, which rise up to the full height of the cathedral and are reminiscent of an ancient Roman

triumphal arch. Halfway up, an eye-catching ledge divides the façade and continues along the rectangular tower on the left-hand side. It is 60 m high, and it was originally intended to be 78 m but remained truncated with a flat covering. The lower part was where Cano had his workshop, a man who was once so famous that he was able at times to pay his creditors with his own sketches.

The *interior* is 116 m in length, 67 m in breadth and consists of five naves and transept. Because you now enter the cathedral from Gran Vía de Colón, your gaze is at once captured by the layered construction of the 48-m-high, domed *Capilla Mayor* with its artistic glass windows from the 16th century.

The conquest of Granada in the name of Cristianity and the expulsion of the last remaining Moors in Europe was the life's work of the most powerful Spanish monarchs, Isabel of Castille and Fernando of Aragón. Because of this, they also wished to be buried here. Their mortal remains have lain buried since 1521 in the Royal Chapel, where they were transported from the Alhambra hill. The same is true of the remains of Juana the Mad (the daughter of the Catholic monarchs) and her Habsburg spouse, Philip the Handsome. They are laid to rest in the crypt in lead coffins covered in leather. In the chapel are the wonderful monumental beds made of Carrara marble, on which the figures are reproduced with touching reality. The double monument for Isabel and Fernando is the work of the Italian sculptor Domenico Fancelli. You can admire Isabel and Fernando's crowns and sceptres in the sacristy next to the burial chamber, where there are also some important works of art, especially by Flemish masters. You reach this part of the cathedral, which was built in 1505–21 by Enrique de Egas in late-gothic style, by passing through the medieval stock market *(lonja)*.

In the 18th century, the *Iglesia del Sagrario* was built as an extension to the cathedral on the site of a former mosque. Legends tell of Hernán Pérez del Pulgar, who it is said, at the time of the besieging of Granada by the Christian forces in 1490, penetrated deep into enemy territory and attached an Ave Maria to the door of the mosque. The present-day church was built in 1705–1759 in baroque style and is home to, as well as its beautiful marble altar, an artistic Renaissance font dating from 1522. *Cathedral: Mon–Sat 10.30 am–1.30 pm and 4 pm–7 pm (in winter: 3.30 pm–6.30 pm), Sun, 4 pm–7 pm; 300 Ptas; Capilla same times; 300 Ptas*

Monasterio de la Cartuja (O)

Of this Carthusian monastery dating from the beginning of the 16th century, the church, sacristy, cloister and refectory remain. The finely worked figure of Saint Bruno on the main altar in the church and the rich stucco ornamentation in the sacristy are extreme examples of the cluttered Spanish Churriguera style. You somehow sense from the atmosphere exuded by the whole complex of this monastery in the north of the city that it has a will of its own. The Carthusian monastery of what was originally an order of recluses became the site of delirious building work, driven on by some mad urge towards extravagance and excess. *In winter: daily 10 am–1 pm (Sun 10 am–midday) and 3.30 pm–6 pm; in summer: daily 10 am–1 pm (Sun 10 am–midday) and 4 pm–7 pm; 300 Ptas; bus route 8; Paseo de la Cartuja*

Sacromonte (U/F2)

🔊 This lofty quarter of the city stretches up the valley of Río Darro behind the quarter of Albaicín. The best way of getting to the holy mountain ("sacro monte") from the city centre is via the Plaza Nueva, the Carrera del Darro and the Cuesta del Chapiz. Then you turn right into the cactus and agave-lined Camino del Sacromonte – and you find yourself in a totally different Granada. Sacromonte is an old gypsy quarter. The origins of the *gitanos* is uncertain. It seems probable that they won the right to settle there as a result of their support for the Christian conquerors during the recapture of Granada. They have now become an indispensible part of the city.

They celebrate the melancholy *cante jondo*, the original song of flamenco, with heart-rendering vividness. Of course, their flamenco performances in cellar bars – frequently at vastly inflated prices – are heavily orientated towards the tourist trade. You usually even have to purchase "permission to photograph". Nothing is achieved by complaining out loud about the blatant commercialisation, the unashamedly criminal prices charged for drinks in some places or the daylight robbery that sometimes occurs during *tablaos flamencos*. It is a much better idea to do your homework before you go, and to avoid the area at night if you are not going as part of a group. The view from the mountain at night of the floodlit Alhambra and the rest of the city down below is especially beautiful.

San Jerónimo (U/B2–3)

★ The monastery stands only a few hundred metres to the north west of the nostalgic Plaza Bib-Rambla with its monumental fountain. In 1496, this was the first place of worship to be consecrated after the expulsion of the Moors. Completed in 1547 by Diego de Siloé, it is one of the finest Renaissance church buildings in Spain, and possesses a wonderful *inner courtyard* with a cloister. *Mon–Sat 10 am–1.30 pm and 4 pm–7.30 pm (winter: 3.30 pm–6 pm), Sun 11am–1.30 pm; 350 Ptas; C. Rector López Argüeta 9*

City of Charles V

To mark the 500th birthday of the king, a tour, either on foot or by minibus, has been organised taking in all the major historical buildings of the period. The guides try to convey the atmosphere of the 16th century, when Charles V lived in Granada. Pre-booking required: *Oficina Carlos V. Centenario; Tel. 958 24 83 81; Fax 958 24 83 82*

MUSEUMS

Lorca-Summerresidence (O)

The poet Federico García Lorca lived in the country, but in Granada he had a summer house that has been opened to visitors. *Tues–Sun 10 am–1 pm and 5 pm–8 pm (in winter 4 pm–7 pm); 300 Ptas; Wed free; Huerta de San Vicente 6*

Museo de la Abadía del Sacromonte (O)

On the holy mountain, works by major Spanish artists, manuscripts from the days of the Arabs and miniature books are

---

In the spirit of Marco Polo

Marco Polo was the first true world traveller. He travelled with peaceful intentions forging links between the East and the West. His aim was to discover the world, and explore different cultures and environments without changing or disrupting them. He is an excellent role model for the travellers of today and the future. Wherever we travel we should show respect for other peoples and the natural world.

WWF

on display, which help to give an insight into the history of the art of printing in Andalusia. *Tues–Sun, 11 am–1 pm and 4 pm–6 pm; 250 Ptas*

Parque de las Ciencias (O)

Opened by the university and sponsored by various banks, this museum is devoted to the latest scientific discoveries, with sections such as the environment, ecology, the throwaway society or the ozone layer. An erosion meter allows you to observe the different effect that rain has on soil with and without plant cover and a telescope permits you to explore events in the sky. There is a special section for children. *Tues–Sat 10 am–7 pm, Sun 10 am–3 pm; 500 Ptas; Av. Mediterráneo s/n; buses 4, 5, 10 and 11*

RESTAURANTS, BARS AND CAFÉS

Alcaicería (U/C3–4)

Intimate restaurant beneath a floral balcony in a small inner courtyard. In the former Moorish bazaar quarter close to the cathedral. Refined Spanish cuisine. *Placeta de la Alcaicería; Tel. 958 22 43 41; daily; category 2*

Bar J. Carlos (O)

✪ Small but fine tapa bar, very popular. *Daily from 2 pm; C. Arabial s/n; category 2*

Chiquito (U/C4)

This place is steeped in history: it was the former watering hole of the literary circle "El Rinconcillo", to which Lorca also belonged. Truly excellent range of food, great choice of tapas. *Pl. del Campillo 9; Tel. 958 22 33 64; closed Wed; category 2*

Colombia (U/E4)

The *restaurante típico* close to the Alhambra combines an interior inspired by Arabic design and Andalusian cuisine. This marvelous atmosphere does come at a price, and this isn't somewhere you could come everyday. *C. Antequeruela Baja 1; Tel. 958 22 74 33; closed Sun; category 2*

Cunini (U/B3)

Gourmets swear that it is the best fish restaurant in Granada. Impressive range of seafood. *Pl. de la Pescadería 9; Tel. 958 25 07 77; closed Mon; category 2*

La Flor del Mar (U/C4)

Fish dishes that are not only very well cooked but also come in a great variety, a rarity in Granada. The proprietors guarantee fresh fish daily. *C. Milagro 5; Tel. 958 52 11 05; closed Sun; category 2*

Gran Café Bib-Rambla (U/C4)

Coffee house in Art Nouveau style opened in 1919 with the old interior, tastefully situated on the lively *Plaza Bib-Rambla 4.*

Helados Jijonenca (U/C5)

People come here to eat ice cream. Recommended are the *turrón*, a splendid nougat ice cream, and the *horchata de chufa*, a delicious almond milk. *Carrera del Genil 97*

Lisboa (U/C3)

🏃 This is where the local youth hangs out. Chatting and flirting is the order of the day. Those whose interests are not erotic feast at the cake counter and on the great view of the Plaza Nueva. *C. Reyes Católicos 65*

Maitena (O)

❖ The most popular out-of-town restaurant with the locals is situated half way into the Sierra. Lamb cutlets and sucking pig are savoured under trees with the Río Genil and the mountains in view. *Estación de Maitena s/n; Güéjar Sierra; Tel. 958 48 41 50; daily; category 2*

Mirador de Morayma (U/E2)

↘ Reasonably priced fare with a view of the Alhambra. The deserts are literally-heavenly, as they were created by the nuns at the Zafra convent. *C. Pianista García Carrillo 2; Tel. 958 22 82 90; closed Sun/Mon; category 2*

Pilar del Toro (U/D3)

Regional cuisine, e.g. *habas a la granadina,* tasty beans with ham. There are many little delights with gorgeous fillings at the bar. *Hospital Santa Ana 12; Tel. 958 22 38 47; daily; category 2*

Samarganda (U/C3)

❖ Restaurant with beautiful terrace in the historical centre. Specialities from the Near East and North Africa, reasonable prices; popular with Grenadines. *Caldería Vieja 3; Tel. 958 21 00 04; daily; category 3*

Las Tinajas (U/B4)

Dark, heavy beams and old-fashioned furniture – but first-class Granadino cuisine. *C. Martínez Campos 17; Tel. 958 25 43 93; daily; category 2*

SHOPPING

Antiques (U/C3)

A small shop, crammed full of old furniture and jewellery that has seen better days. *La Diligencia. C. Reyes Católicos 63*

Flamenco instruments (U/E5)

In addition to classical instruments, *Montero* also produces hand-made concert guitars starting from 150,000 Ptas. *Cuesta del Caidero 1*

Ceramics (U/D3)

Cerámica al-Yarrar has a range of Arab ceramics in beautiful colours and patterns. *C. Bañuelo 5*

Arts and Crafts

Handicrafts, including work by agricultural workers from the Alpujarras, are to be found in the *Corral del Carbón* (**U/C4**) at the *Asociación de Artesanos del Albaicín.* This former caravanserai is the oldest surviving relic from the Moorish epoch and served as both hostel and market place. In the inner court were the stables for horses and other load-bearing animals, and which have now been converted into market stalls, whilst the traders reside in the floor above. This complex is now home to *artespaña,* an association of artistic craftspeople. The original inlaid work by *Taller de Artesanía Árabe* (**U/E2,** *Cuesta del Chapiz 7*) is a good example of fine artistic craftwork.

Leather

Well-made belts, bags and other leather products are available at *Eduardo Ferrer Lucena* (**U/D1–2,** *C. Agua del Albaicín 19*). Hand-made riding tack is to be found at *Guarnicionería Jandones* (**U/B3,** *C. Jaudenes*).

Fashion (U/C3–4)

Cortefiel is a giant fashion house in a neo-baroque building, whose façade is floodlit at night (*Pl. de Is-*

abel la Católica/Gran Vía de Colón). *Pupus (C. Monrería 7)* stocks high-class fashion by star designers. *Stadium (Placeta de Santo Cristo 2)* is a well-stocked shop specialising in the newest looks for men with stylish shirts and jackets. Just next door is *Amore Mujer (Placeta de Santo Cristo 4),* with classical Spanish women's fashion. *Catimini (Arco de las Orejas s/n)* reveals itself on closer inspection to be an amusingly laid out shop for children's clothing. *Limón (C. Zacatín 20A)* is a good place to look for reasonably priced evening wear among other things, while *Spaghetti (C. Zacatín 23)* is the place for all kinds of clothes. If you need reasonably priced business suits, a good place to make for is *Gales (C. Zacatín 15A).* At *Francisco Trabado (C. Zacatín 24A),* a well-established hat shop, a señora advises men on the subject of headwear. *Stradivarini (C. Mesones 30)* has a slightly offbeat range for the young and young at heart.

Shoes   (U/B4)

High-class goods in the style of the south at affordable prices at *Julio Callejón, C. Mesones 36.*

Souvenirs   (U/C3–4)

In the shade of the cathedral, the *Alcaicería* seems to be fertile ground for kitsch. Here you will find row upon row of little shops and stalls peddling every conceivable variation on the theme of flamenco feathers, pendants, castanets, and many other bright and colourful, but useless, wares. This was originally the Moorish silk market and it still forms a pleasing architectonic whole today, retaining something of the oriental souk atmosphere.

ACCOMMODATION

Albergue Juvenil Viznar   (O)

This youth hostel equipped with its own swimming pool is set in the mountains 7 km above Granada. *108 beds; Camino de Fuente Grande s/n; 18179 Viznar; Tel. 958 54 33 07; Fax 958 54 34 48*

Alixares del Generalife   (U/F4)

Hotel with pool and piano bar in one of the most famous gardens of the world. *170 rooms; Av. de los Alixares; Tel. 958 22 55 75; Fax 958 22 41 02; category 2–3*

América   (U/E 4)

Cosy hotel with only 13 rooms and a friendly atmosphere. Breakfast is served on a typical Andalusian patio. *Real de la Alhambra 53; Tel. 958 22 74 71; Fax 958 22 74 70; category 2*

Camping Reina Isabel   (O)

Probably the best-run campsite in the vicinity of Granada. A further attraction is the great view of the Alhambra and Sierra Nevada. *171 Places; all year; Ctra. de Zubia; 4 km outside city; Tel. 958 59 00 41; Fax 958 59 11 91*

Casablanca   (U/E 2)

Simple *hotel residencia* with plenty of brass and sumptuous fabrics. The prices are unbeatable. *49 rooms; C. Frailes 5; Tel. 958 25 76 00; Fax 958 26 67 58; category 3*

Gran Vía Granada   (U/C3)

The postmodern building stands on one of the principal arteries of the city. Marble is very much in evidence, and there is a underground car park. The large ❖

✝ restaurant is very popular with locals and young people owing to the reasonably priced fare. *85 rooms; Gran Vía de Colón 25; Tel. 958 28 54 64; Fax 958 28 55 91; category 2–3*

Macía Plaza (U/C3)

Simple hotel right in the middle of things, fitted out in Andalusian style. *44 rooms; Pl. Nueva 4; Tel. 958 22 75 36; Fax 958 22 75 33; category 3*

Las Nieves (U/B4)

Reasonably priced hotel in the lower part of the city. The lady of the house herself cooks for her guests. *30 rooms; C. Sierpe Baja 5; Tel. 958 26 53 11; Fax 958 52 31 95; category 3*

Palacio de Santa Inés (U/D2)

Palace dating from the 16th century in Albaicín, with colourful frescoes and roofed inner courtyard. Not expensive. *13 rooms; Cuesta de Santa Inés 9; Tel. 958 22 23 62, Fax 958 22 24 65; category 1*

Parador de Granada San Francisco (U/E4)

Take the opportunity to stay in a former convent, built on the orders of Isabella of Castille. The guests at the palace, restored in 1995, enjoy the privilege of experiencing the Alhambra at night and in the early morning when there are no tourists. *36 rooms; Real de la Alhambra; Tel. 958 22 14 40; Fax 958 22 22 64; category 1*

The Parador on the Alhambra hill: no chance without reservation

Los Tilos (U/C4)

Simple hotel, but in a perfect location and with a famous café right next door. You only have to set one foot out of the door and you are in the middle of the hustle and bustle of Granada. *24 rooms; Pl. Bib-Rambla 4; Tel. 958 26 67 12; Fax 958 26 68 01; category 3*

SPANISH COURSES

✠ In Granada, there are Spanish courses lasting several weeks and aimed primarily at young people – the best way of getting to know the country and its people. Further details in several languages are available from *Información Juvenil*, (**U/C4**) *C. Varela 4; Tel. 958 22 20 53*. Another very attractive and effective way of getting to know the locals is to study alongside them at the *Escuela Montalbán*, ten minutes on foot from the city centre. At this institution, foreigners learn Spanish and Spaniards learn foreign languages in the room next door; the campus is polyglott. The courses have a strictly practical orientation and cover all levels from beginner to advanced. The mornings are devoted to swotting and the excursions are serious affairs.

SPORTS & EXCURSIONS

Mountaineering (U/A5)

The *Federación Andaluza de Montañismo* allows mountaineers to contact one another and organises excursions. *Camino de Ronda 101, Edificio Atalaya 1, oficina 76, 18003 Granada; Tel./Fax 958 29 13 40*

Flamenco courses (U/F4)

In the historical city centre, the uninitiated are taken through their fast, stamping paces by professionals. Five-day intensive course from 28,900 Ptas with accommodation. *Carmen de las Cuevas, Cuesta de los Chinos 15, 18010 Granada; Tel. 958 22 10 62; Fax 958 22 04 76*

Golf (O)

There is an 18-hole course 10 km from the city at *Las Gabias (Tel./Fax 958 58 44 36; 5,000 Ptas, after 3 pm 3,000 Ptas)*.

Riding (O)

Excursions lasting one or several days in the Sierra Nevada, through the Alpujarras, to the Costa Granadina and right as far as Almería. Accomodation is provided at guest houses and at *cortijos*, country estates. *Cabalgar Rutas Alternativas, Rafael Belmonte, 18412 Bubión; Tel./Fax 958 76 31 35*

Bullfighting (O)

This bloodthirsty spectacle takes place on Sundays in the warmest months of the year and the most important fights are in June. This is where to see the Andalusians living out one of their great passions. A place in the shade will set you back up to 4,000 Ptas, in the sun about 1,000 Ptas. *Pl. de Toros, Av. Doctor Olóriz 25*

Tennis (U/A5)

Pistas de Tenis Neptuno, C. Arabial s/n; Tel. 958 25 10 55; 800 Ptas per hour

Winter sports (U/A4)

Information about winter sports can be obtained from the *Federación Andaluza de Deportes de In-*

vierno. Av. de Cervantes 21, 18003 Granada; Tel. 958 13 57 48

ENTERTAINMENT

Café-Pub Amadeus (U/A3)

This is the place if you want to meet members of the opposite sex. Disco and pub in one, reasonably priced drinks. *Daily 8 pm–3 am; C. Pintor López Mezquita 14*

Caldereria Nueva (U/C3)

☀ This exhaust-fume-free alley in the Albaicín is very popular due to the large number of pubs that it boasts and the reasonably priced tea rooms and bars. During the warm three-quarters of the year chairs stand out on the well-trodden paving stones and cats dart by amongst the legs of those seated. Here, the most amusing bars: *A Zahara (No. 12),* where incense hangs in the air and you sip at Maghreb mint tea in surroundings reminiscent of a souk; *Teteria Alfaguara (No. 7),* which serves fruit juices and milk drinks as well as Asian teas; *Teteria as Surat (No. 5),* with carpeted walls and lanterns that emit a dim light reminiscent of the thousand and one nights, small tables engraved with verses from the Koran, Arabic songs and staff from North Africa *Teteria Café (No. 24),* where you sit on low stools in front of flat tables to drink tea and oriental sweets.

Calle Pedro Antonio de Alarcón (U/A3-5)

☀ Street with a high concentration of pubs and bars, which are packed full, mostly with young people, every night. This street, along with its side streets, is the main centre of student nocturnal social life. Beer on tap *(caña),* a glass of red wine and tapas are generally cheap.

Casa Enrique (U/C4)

In existence as a tapa bar for more than 100 years. Accompanied by a glass of Andalusian wine you can work your way through the little treats. *Acera del Darro 8*

Castaneda (U/C3)

❧ Large bar, bursting at the seams every evening, brings together academics and business people who feast on the opulent ham and cheese dishes washed down with good wine. Loud, busy, authentic. *Placeta de San Gil 6/C. Elvira*

La Castellana (U/C4)

You are served a tapa together with your drink, and then you can enjoy them whilst allowing your gaze to wander around the mirrored bar as it darts from your own image to that of fellow guests. *C. Angel Ganivet 2*

Flamenco and Folklore

Not everything that is peddled in Granada under the guise of flamenco is the real McCoy. Particularly in the whitewashed gypsy caves of Sacromonte, Andalusian folklore is often performed without real feeling. It takes a fair bit of luck to stumble on a performance that still conveys something of the power and naturalness of Flamenco. *Jardines Neptuno* (**U/A5**) in the *C. Arabial s/n; Tel. 958 25 11 12*, is an address worth noting: the choreographic director of the group is Mariquilla, a professor of "Flamencology".

A number of organisations offer special package deals to hotel guests: transport by coach with multilingual guide, a brief nighttime tour, dinner at a typical hotel, followed by a flamenco show. After midnight, the party is brought back to their hotels. Reservations: *Sala Príncipe, Campo del Príncipe 7; Tel. 958 22 80 88; Los Tarantos,* *Sacromonte 9; Tel. 958 22 45 25; Tablao Reina Mora, Mirador de San Cristóbal; Tel. 958 27 82 28.* Bookings can also be made at most hotels. The cost of these tours is in the region of 4,000–7,000 Ptas.

Granada 10 (U/C3)

♣ Gigantic disco where you can dance until you drop, always chock-a-block. Women get in for nothing more than a smile in the direction of the staff on the door, the admission price for men is 1,000 Ptas. *Mon–Sat 10 pm–4 am; C. Cárcel Baja 10*

Cinema

The latest releases are shown at the *Astoria* (**U/B1**, *Av. de la Constitución*), there is a complex with eight cinemas at the *Multicentro* (**U/B4**, *Solarillo de Gracia 9–11*), and there are three cinemas at the *Centro Comercial* (**U/B4**, *C. Recogidas 4*).

La Tertulia (U/A3)

❖ Night bar where the passionate tango dancers of Granada are to be seen strutting their stuff. *C. Pintor López Mezquita*

The city centre of Granada: the place for those who come alive at night

Oficina de Turismo

(**U/C4**) *Pl. de Mariana Pineda 10, 18012 Granada; Tel./Fax 95822 66 88;* (**U/C4**) *Corral del Carbón, 18001 Granada; Tel. 958 22 59 90; Fax 958 22 89 18.* For anyone who is staying at a hotel in the city, the tourist association provides free tours to nearby places of interest (cave dwellings at Guadix, Thermal baths at Alhama, Alpujarras etc.). Information and reservations at the Oficina de Turismo.

Casa Museo de Federico García Lorca in Fuente Vaqueros (107/D2)

This house, birthplace of the great man, has virtually become a place of pilgrimage. Classes of schoolchildren, students, and also ordinary country people make the 20-kilometre journey to the northwest of Granada. Federico García Lorca (1898–1936) is considered to be probably the most significant Spanish poet of the 20th century. His powerful use of language and sense of rhythm have influenced generations of poets and millions of readers. The documents of a short life that ended tragically have been brought together in the house of Lorca's parents. The poet, who always felt an affinity for ordinary people, especially gypsies, and always declared that he had no interest in politics, was shot in the small village of Viznar near Granada by supporters of Franco and buried. His corpse has not been found to this day. The pictures, furniture, the scrawled, ink-stained manuscripts and the atmosphere of the house speak volumes about the poet. *April–June:*

Tues–Sun 10 am–1 pm and 5 pm–7 pm; July–Sept: 10 am–1 pm and 6 pm–8 pm; Oct–Mar: 10 am–1 pm and 4 pm–6 pm; 200 Ptas; C. Poeta García Lorca 4; During the day, there is an hourly bus service from the station in Granada, Av. de Andaluces

Galera (O)

The village (pop. 1,600) in the north of the province of Granada, set between mountains and nature parks, is some 150 km from Granada. This journey will pay dividends to those who are in search of unusual holiday experiences in the country. For here, in the green valley between two rivers, is the only place in Spain where you can stay in cave accomodation. The soft stone stays pleasantly cool in summer and retains the heat in winter. The caves are equipped with electricity and running water. This trip is especially to be recommended to hikers, who can try out the ten routes prepared by the tourist office in Galera, taking in places of interest in the local countryside. It is also possible to employ a guide, rent a donkey or rent a bicycle. This is the perfect tonic for those seeking a change of scenery to something less hectic after the touristic shunting yard of the Alhambra. The inhabitants of Galera are hospitable and open to outsiders, the wine cellars offer good samples of the local produce, and there are substantial portions of meat or vegetable stews in the hostelries. The price per day of a stay at the cave accomodation ranges between 12,000 Ptas (four people) and 18,000 Ptas (eight people), minimum stay two nights. *(Information and Bookings: Promociones Turísticas de Galera, C. Cervantes 11, 18840 Galera; Tel./ Fax*

The cave dwellings at Guadix resemble a surreal film set

958739068). There is a cave hotel that lives up to its name 10 km further east near *Orce (Laveranda; 8 rooms; C. Fuentenueva s/n; Tel./Fax 958 34 43 80; category 3)*.

Guadix (108/A2)

Approximately 5,000 inhabitants of this town (pop. 20,000) live in underground cave dwellings. The steep slopes of loess, which allow for easy excavation, have always been used as dwellings. Nowadays the cave dwellings are marked by their white outer walls, chimneys rising up from the ground and antennae. The most interesting cave settlements are to be found 6 km to the north west of the city in *Purullena*. It is not easy to get a look at one of these dwellings in the *barrio troglodita*. If you find yourself spontaneously invited in, it is worth first checking whether any kind of financial remuneration is expected. Guadix was first founded by the Romans under Julius Caesar. The Moors built a *fortress*, which is open to visitors *(daily 9 am–1 pm and 4 pm–6 pm; 200 Ptas)*. The ↘ hill affords the best view of the bizarre landscape of hills and caves with the remains of the town wall. The

best restaurant in the town, *Hotel Comercio (Mira de Amezcua 3; Tel. 958 66 05 00; daily; category 2–3)*, serves the speciality of lamb with honey.

Loja (106/C3)

The white houses of this town (pop. 20,000) stand on a slope sinking down to the Río Genil. Loja is an archetypal Andalusian town which is famous for its romantic alleys. On a hilltop stand the towering, well-preserved remains of the Moorish *Alcazaba* dating from the 10th century. Of the buildings in the town, the two churches are worth seeing: *San Gabriel* (1552) with its spire roof and *Santa María* (16th century) with its baroque façade. Some 20 km to the west is the luxurious hotel complex *La Bobadilla (Apartado 144, 18300 Loja; 62 rooms; Tel. 958 32 18 61; Fax 958 32 18 10; category 1)*, which is based on a concept combining the typical features of an Andalusian village with the historically authentic architectural forms of the Mudejar style (mixture of Moorish and Christian architecture). The reception building is a pillared lobby which has a mosque-like feel to it, all the rooms are furnished with antique rustic Andalusian furniture and have marble floors and marble-clad bathrooms, fountains babble in the peaceful inner courtyard. All ◁▷ rooms have sun terraces and afford a view far over the hilly terrain. Restaurant with international cuisine.

SIERRA NEVADA

(107/E-F3-4) The mountain range lying to the south east of Granada is the highest on the Iberian peninsula. The cold, dry Sierra wind blows its way through the wild landscape with its massive rock formations, and it is almost impossible to believe that you are only about 60 km from the shores of the Mediterranean. Above 2,000 m the fine-leafed cushion plants disappear and the thorny bushes clinging to the slopes are all that remains as far as plant life goes. On a clear day you can make out the African coast and the straits Gibraltar from the roof of Andalusia. Snow is normally guaranteed in Europe's southernmost skiing region from December until April. The journey up to the peaks, more than 3,000 m high, from the pleasant Mediterranean climate to a region where in places there is permanent snow is an experience taking in a great variety of different landscapes.

PLACES IN THE SIERRA NEVADA

Las Alpujarras (107/E-F4, 108/A3-4)

★ Like massive waves the mountains with their sparse vegetation roll down to the Mediterranean. The south of the Sierra Nevada is where the highest settlements in Spain are to be found. They all cling to steep mountain slopes and face south. The cube-shaped houses with their flat roofs made of slate-like, waterproof magnesium aluminate are characteristic of the region. The houses are stacked up together in terrace form and complement each other, with the roof of one serving as the terrace for the one above. This architectonic legacy of the Arabs is particularly evident in the central region along the C 333 highway: *Lanjarón* (trout stream and lovely thermal bath; *Tel. 958 77 01 37; Mar–Dec), Órgiva, Cañar* (tiny village with well-preserved houses in Moorish style, surrounded by woods of oak, chestnut and pine), *Pampaneira* and *Bubión* (both settlements in a lush valley with vegetable gardens, pastures, walnut and chestnut trees), *Capileira, Trevélez* (at a height of 1,580 m, in a deep, tree-filled valley, plenty of trout in the mountain streams), *Pórtugos, Bérchules* and *Ugíjar.*

In contrast to the northern side of the Sierra Nevada, the southern Alpujarras seem more natural. A wild mountainous landscape that only permits people to settle on its southern slopes. After the conquest by the Christians, peasants from Galicia were settled here, a reserved, taciturn folk lacking in temperament. As far as the Andalusians are concerned, this area was considered well into the 20th century to be bewitched. If you come in the autumn to these often hidden villages with the lowest per capita income in Spain and a shockingly high rate of illiteracy, you can participate in the *murraca,* the chestnut harvest or the apple

In Bubión you can rent one of the typical bungalows

harvest and in the process gain an impression of how the fields were worked in days gone by, using mules and strong oxen.

Between Capileira and Pampaneira are situated the *Villas Turísticas de Bubión (Tel. 958 76 31 12; Fax 958 76 31 36; category 2)*: 43 bungalows in the Alpujarreño style. *Dallas Love Sierra Trails* in *Pampaneira (C. Verónica s/n; Tel./Fax 958 76 30 38)* rents out land rovers and organises riding tours. Food with a strong rustic flavour is served at *Lanjarón* in *El Club (Av. Andalucía 16–18; Tel. 958 77 01 53; category 3)*. In *Capileira* the *Mesón Poqueira (C. Doctor Castilla; Tel. 958 76 30 48; Oct–Mar: closed Mon; category 3)* is a family enterprise specialising in meat dishes. In *Trevélez* you can dine at ✦ *Mesón la Fragua (C. San Antonio 4; Tel. 958 85 85 73; category 3)* where you can enjoy partridge, rabbit, lamb or trout whilst taking in the view.

If you have the urge to bring back something tasty with you, get some *jamón serrano,* the famous spiced ham, in one of the villages.

It is dried for more than a year in the high alpine air and has a mature aroma. A kilo costs 1,000–1,500 Ptas, depending on how long it has been dried, the decisive factor for quality.

Private accomodation in the Pueblos der Alpujarras can be booked using the common reservation centre shared by the providers of such accomodation: *RAAR (Red Andaluza de Alojamientos Rurales),* a non-commercial service: *Apartado de Correos 2035, 04080 Almería; Tel. 950 26 50 18; Fax 950 27 04 31; www.raar.es.* If you book for at least two days, you will be accommodated with a family and have the chance to see something of the daily life on the land (bed and breakfast or half-board are both available). This holiday accommodation can be anywhere from a traditional house in the middle of nowhere with no electricity to a comfortable mansions. Most of the accommodation on offer falls into price category 3. Those who prefer to stay in a hotel should try the *Taray Alpujarra* in *Órgiva (26 rooms; Ctra. Tablate-Al-buñol; 18 km; Tel. 958 78 45 25; Fax 958 78 45 31; category 2)*, a modern hotel in the classical Moorish style with pool, or in *Cádiar das Alquería de Morayma (9 rooms; Ctra. Cádiar-Torvíscón; Tel./Fax 958 34 32 21; category 3)*, an old leasehold farm which has been modernised. Since it was opened in 1995, the *Alcazaba de Busquístar* in *Busquístar (Ctra. Órgiva-Laujar; km 37; Tel. 958 85 86 87; Fax 958 85 86 93; category 2)* which has been preserved in the traditional Alpajarras style has been dubbed the best hotel in the region. No expense has been spared in fitting out the 46 rooms, there is a gaming room and a heated swimming pool.

There is a daily coach tour of the Alpujarras from Granada *(Tel. 958 22 59 90)*.

Mulhacén/Pico de Veleta (107/F3)

In the summer, the Sierra Nevada is one of the regions with the most pleasant climate in Spain. If you leave the road from Granada to the coast at km 27 you will find yourself on a twisting country road and continuing for a further 25 km you pass through Lanjarón and near the settlement of Pampaneira you find, forking off to the left, the highest mountain road in Europe (only passable in summer). The roadway twists and turns its way up to *Laguna de la Caldera,* a crystal clear mountain lake at a height of 2,800 m. This corrie filled with melted snow is a popular starting point for hikes to the *Mulhacén,* the highest mountain on the Spanish mainland (3,482 m). Even those of us who are not mountaineers can, if they are in reasonably good condition, make the climb in 60 min-

utes. Real outdoor types can camp at the blue and green shimmering lagoon. Temperatures fall below freezing at night. If your tyres are up to it, you can bump up and down all the way to ❊ *Pico de Veleta* (3398 m). At the summit, on a pyramid of crudely cut stones stands the "anorexic" *Virgen de las Nieves,* a statue of the Virgin Mary with a child wrapped in a coat.

Ski resort Solynieve/Pradollano (107/F3)

This area, a mere 32 km south east of Granada, with the 2,100-m-high, central town of Pradollano has, since the slopes of the Veleta were discovered by skiers, turned into a boom town at altitude with modern hotels and apartment blocks and a total of 12,000 beds for visitors. The town has been created out of nothing to radiate in a practical way around the Plaza Andalucía making it easy to find your way around. The place owes its special charms to the *joie de vivre* of the Spaniards who have built up a nightlife here that is famous throughout the Iberian peninsula.

The 2,500-hectare skiing area has 34 pistes with a total length of 61 km. A choice of 20 lifts mean that you never have to wait long. The runs are well prepared and safe. There are no avalanches or crevasses. This makes it an ideal place for beginners. In addition to deep snow slopes and cross country trails, there are also slopes for snowboarders. At a height of 2,230 m is the High Performance Athletic Training Centre. You can rent ski trainers and mountain guides here. The season begins at the end of November and continues until mid–April. Should strong sunshine lead to a lack of snow even in winter, 200 snow cannons start firing at full blast. One interesting side-effect of the hectic nightlife here is that most of the Spaniards sleep in until noon, with the result that the pistes are pleasantly empty in the mornings. The mountain range on the same latitude as Tunisia is only an hour away from the Mediterranean. In places you can see its blue sparkle as you ski down. A ski pass costs 3,500 Ptas, information about snow and weather conditions is available on *Tel. 958 24 91 00* and *958 48 01 53*. Skis can be rented for a week at prices starting from approximately 10,000 Ptas and there are also skiing schools.

The Moors were the first people to take an interest in the snowy mountains. In the summer they would bring ice down from the mountains and use it to keep their food cool. The necessary infrastructure for sport in the Sierra Nevada wasn't set up until after World War II. The region is a paradise for hikers, lovers of botany and children. With its area of 86,000 sq m, the largest national park in Spain is populated by martens, foxes and badgers, whilst golden eagles hover above. There are roughly 800 species of Alpine flora which are unique to this area.

For help in finding accommodation, contact the *Central de Reservas Sierra Nevada Club (Agencia de Viajes; Tel. 958 24 91 11; Fax 958 48 06 06)*. We recommended the hotel *Meliá Sierra Nevada (221 rooms; Pl. de Pradollano s/n; Tel. 958 48 04 00; Fax 958 48 04 58; closed Apr–Nov; category 1)*. As well as renting out winter sport equipment, ski courses are also available. The most exclusive restaurant in Pradollano is *Ruta del Veleta (Ctra. de Sierra Nevada;*

km 5.4.; Tel. 958 48 61 34; category 1–2) with Andalusian specialities. Other good establishments are *Casablanca (Tel. 958 48 11 05; category 2)* and the family-friendly *Pizzeria Floren (Edificio Primavera II; Tel. 958 48 08 52; category 3)*. You can get yourself into the mood for the nightlife in the *Crescendo Lodge* at the valley station of the Genil chairlift and at the *Genil Lodge* beneath the middle station. The hard core congregates at midnight in pubs and discos like *Chimenea, Golpe, Mango, Chiclet* and *Sticky Fingers*.

Other activities: paragliding with the *Draco Paragliding Club (Tel. 958 48 85 60)*. Fitness at the *Club Deportivo Trevenque* with tennis, squash, gymnasium, massages, sauna and a pool *(Edificio Montebajo, Pl. de Andalucía; Tel. 958 48 09 09; daily pass winter 3,000, summer 900 Ptas)*. Leaflets help explore the mountainous terrain under their own steam.

Another good way of exploring the Sierra Nevada is on a mountain bike, making your way day by day along gravel tracks and mule paths up to heights of 800 metres. The ideal destination is Cabo de Gata near Almería, the best time of year is spring or autumn. Prices start from 85,000 Ptas. per week with half-board and transportation of luggage. Bookings at *Ciclo Montana Espana, Camino Real 3, Barranco Ferrer, Rubite 18711, Granada; Tel/Fax +34 958 349115; www.tuspain.com/ciclo*.

The *Bonal-Bus* leaves Granada daily (departure from the Av. de la Constitución at 9 am, return at 5 pm). Tickets in the bar *El Ventorillo* beside the Palacio de Congreso *(Tel. 958 27 31 00)*. A taxi costs around 4,000 Ptas.

Africa in Europe

*Villages as white as chalk, a real desert:
the wallflower awakens*

The east of Andalusia is as white as chalk. Many villages here look like Berber settlements transplanted onto European soil from the high Atlas mountains. The only thing missing are the minarets. In the isolated villages of the sparse uplands, set amongst dunes reminiscent of a desert and fields of esparto grass, in plains bathed in light and in a grey moon landscape with a hint of earthly greens and browns, the modern way of calculating time is only just beginning to gain acceptance. The terraces of tropical fruit trees stretch from mountains 2,000 metres high to the Mediterranean. With more than 3,000 hours of sun per year, the coastal region between Almuñécar and Almería is one of the sunniest spots on the Mediterranean. No other region of Europe is able to match the productivity of its agriculture. Especially in the flat western approaches to the Sierra de Gádor huge greenhouses wrapped in sheets of plastic stretch out for kilometres. The fertile fields border directly on dry areas which are reminiscent of the Wild West and were used as the film set

The favourite resort of the Granadino: Salobreña with its contorted maze of alleys and flights of steps

for classics such as *Laurence of Arabia* and several westerns. The Sierra de Alhamilla is the only desert in Europe.

It has taken the locals a long time to wake up to the economic dimension of tourism. Even so, the region still seems happy to serve mainly as the springboard to the continent over the water, as the existence of regular ferries to Morocco shows. Because of its geographical and spiritual orientation, the Spanish writer Juan Goytisolo named the province of Almería, poor in works of art but rich in sunshine, "Africa in Europe".

ALMERÍA

(108/C4) A notorious den of pirates has become one of the major harbours of Spain. Even in the Middle Ages there was a great deal of commercial shipping activity, and nowadays the goods are mainly ores, fish and fruit. Almería (pop. 160, 000) used to be the scene of great friction between the sea robbers who thronged here and the land-based legionnaires. The town was conquered, lost, reconquered, surrendered once more and incorporated into numerous anarchistic realms. Many of the fortifications from the wild past have been preserved until this day – the

53

cathedral itself was more than just a secure stronghold of God. In comparison to the towns in the west of the Costa del Sol, Almería has a run down feel to it, although the fact that everything here is tainted with the odium of shabbiness actually lends the place a certain charm. You sense that beneath the surface the whole history of the town has been preserved layer by layer. The older parts of the town below the Alcazaba, particularly the old Arab Quarter, are full of particularly picturesque alleys and snug little corners. Bar follows bar, for Almería has an excessive love of nightlife. And at night, the alleys and squares are filled with noise and thronged full of groups wandering from pub to pub in search of tapas. Here, in contrast to Granada, the little morsels are more likely to contain seafood. The *almerienses* are masters of the art of frying salted fish and grilling sea snails, gambas and rings of octopus, all spiced with garlic.

SIGHTS

Alcazaba

★ As far as fortifications of this size go, this is one of the most impressive whose origins date back to the time of the Moors, with an enclosed area of 35,335 sq m, 91 m above sea level. This area was large enough to give sanctuary to 20,000 people within the safety of its three rings of walls. Construction began in 955 under the founder of the town, Abdarrahman III. Following damage by earthquakes and wars, the fortifications were rebuilt many times by successive Muslim and Christian rulers. A *garden* has been laid out behind the first ring of walls

and it is a pleasant place to take a walk. The *watchtower* dates back from the time of the Bourbon king Charles III. Behind the second ring the remains of former palaces are to be seen. In the place where today a chapel in Mudejar style stands there was once a mosque. The third ring of the fortifications was built by Castilian conquerors and the *Torre del Homenaje* possesses a late Gothic portal. It is worth making the climb up the ◀️ *Calle Almanzor* near to the Plaza Vieja partly for the view afforded of the town, harbour and surrounding countryside, and also because it takes you into a part of the fortifications that has been restored in exemplary fashion so that you feel as if you have been transported into a fairy-tale world amongst the battlements. *In summer daily 10 am–2 pm and 4.30 pm–8 pm, in winter 9.30 am–2 pm and 4.30 pm–7 pm, admission: 250 Ptas*

Almedina (historical centre)

The *Plaza Vieja* with the pleasing arches of its arcade is the starting point for a visit to the historical centre, with the sophisticated shopping street *Calle de las Tiendas* at its very heart. The street along the sea front, *Parque Nicolás Salmerón* with its palm trees and water jets is a great place to take a stroll. The main street *Paseo de Almería* is dominated by cafés and shops. The route through the Almedina passes several religious buildings. The *Iglesia de Santiago* (16th century, *C. de las Tiendas*) church has a splendid Renaissance gate with the coat of arms of the bishop and a depiction of an impassioned saint. It is also worth seeing (and photographing) the pretty little neo-Moorish *railway*

MARCO POLO SELECTION: ALMERÍA AND THE EAST

1 Alcazaba in Almería
This massive fortified area above the town once gave sanctuary to as many as 20 000 people – a work of generations that took centuries to complete (page 54)

2 Almuñécar
Modernised, yet without spoiling the old charm – an enchanting little town with white houses and picturesque marina on the Costa Tropical (page 57)

---

station, situated just outside the historical centre in the *Ctra. de Ronda Cathedral.*

Cathedral

Gothic and Renaissance dating from the 16th century on the foundations of a mosque. A mixture of castle and fortified church. The massive construction with the four bulky towers has seen tough times and it frequently sustained damage from attacks by Moorish pirates. These constant threats meant that it wasn't unusual for weapons to be stored here. Even the hexagonal apse looks much more like a defensive tower. *Daily 8.30 am–midday and 5.30 pm–8 pm; Pl. Bendicho*

RESTAURANTS

El Bello Rincón

❖ Unpretentious atmosphere but always packed full with locals who know that this is the place in town for excellent fish and seafood. *N 340; 436 km; Tel. 950 23 84 27; closed Mon; category 2*

Casa Puga

One of the most traditional tapa bars on the coast, wide range on offer. *C. Jovellanos 7; Tel. 950 23 15 30; closed Sun; category 3*

Club de Mar

❖ You dine (preferably fish dishes) on a terrace with a fine view of the harbour. *C. de las Almadrabillas 1; Tel. 950 23 50 48; daily; category 2*

SHOPPING

Cuero

Leather goods from inland farm houses. *C. Pedro Jover 26*

Madera

Original wood and basketwork and patchwork covers *(jarapas)* from the Alpujarras. *C. Israel 8*

Mercasa

Old covered market in the *Circunvalación del Mercado.* Very lively, bewitching smell of fresh fish, stands groaning with fruit and vegetables. *Mon–Sat 8 am–2 pm*

ACCOMMODATION

Camping La Garrofa

80 places, on the N 340 to Motril, 435 km; Tel. 950 23 57 70

Costasol

This well-run establishment is located between the town centre and the harbour, you can easily get everywhere on foot. *55 rooms; Paseo de Almería 58; Tel./Fax 950 23 40 11; category 3*

Gran Hotel Almería

◀✹▶ The best hotel in town, with underground garage and swimming pool amongst its facilities. Most rooms have a view of the harbour and sea. *117 rooms and suites; Av. Reina Regente 8; Tel. 950 23 80 11; Fax 950 27 06 9; category 1-2*

Staying in the country

Red Andaluza de Alojamientos Rurales (04080 Almería, Apartado 2035; Tel. 950 26 50 18; Fax 950 27 16 78) acts as an agent for suppliers of accommodation up-country and can supply the "Guía Anual de Turismo Rural" to help you make your choice. This is a particularly good idea for families and groups, who pay something in the region of 34,000–51,000 Ptas to rent a house for a week.

SPORTS & EXCURSIONS

Diving

Information about diving and underwater photography for beginners and experts is available from the *Centro de Actividades Náuticas (Playa de las Almadrabillas 10; Tel. 950 27 06 12; Fax 950 25 21 13).*

Hiking

The *Walking Safari Company (54 High Street East, Uppingham, LE15 9PZ, UK; Tel. 01572 823820)* organises special ✪ guided hiking tours of the peaceful regions of Andalusia, from the desert region around Almería across the green

Historical centre and harbour in Almería: a paradise for pub crawls and tapas tours

Sierras near Ronda with its villages up to the snow covered peaks of Sierra Nevada. You need to be in reasonably good condition to attempt one of these tours. The participants stay in simple hotels, farmhouses and tented camps. Guides are Hugh and Jane Arhithnott, who spent eight years exploring this countryside and have discovered routes previously known only to muleteers and shepherd boys.

Water sports

You can take sailing lessons in the *Club del Mar (C. Muelle 1; Tel. 950 23 07 80),* where there is also a tennis school. The neighbouring town of Roquetas de Mar is home to the *Club Marítimo Roquetas de Mar:* Sailing school, canoeing, swimming (also tennis). *Port Area; Tel. 950 32 29 09*

ENTERTAINMENT

Almería, with almost 200 bars, has the highest density of pubs in the whole of Spain, a fact which stamps its mark on the nightlife of the town. The action is concentrated in the area between Paseo de Almería, Alcazaba and the seafront road Parque Nicolás de Salmerón. There are discos in Aguadulce and the other seaside resorts.

INFORMATION

Oficina de Turismo
Parque Nicolás Salmerón; Tel. 950 27 43 55; Fax 950 27 43 60

SURROUNDING AREA

Aguadulce   (108/C4)
This large resort 13 km west of Almería represents the region's number one bid to get into the

quality tourism market. The hotels and restaurants are up to the task of meeting more refined standards, the beach is fine and sandy, and thanks to its cleanliness and the quality of its water, the blue flag awarded by the EU for exemplary ecological effort flutters proudly in the breeze.

ALMUÑÉCAR

(107/E5) ★ The inhabitants of Almuñécar (pop. 20,000), founded by the Phoenicians and nestling on a foothill of the Sierra de Almijara, earn their living principally from fruit grown in greenhouses and from tourism. The climate is consistently warm and is ideal for sugar cane, avocados, papayas, bananas, mangoes and medlars. The summer lasts for ten months, the autumn, two – and they only experience winter by looking up into the snow-covered heights of the Sierra Nevada three thousand metres up above. These very mountains protect the area from the influence of cold weather from the north. There is something enchanting about the old world Almuñécar, with its white, cube-shaped houses, its twisting alleys and the morning market, that even the frenzied building activity of recent years has been unable to spoil. The beaches are sandy in places, in others pebbly and rocky. The modern marina, Marina del Este looks really picturesque in its rocky bay and shows that not all touristic architecture has to be ugly.

SIGHTS

Stroll around the town
Not to be missed are the remains of a Roman *Aquaduct,* exposed

The charming town of Almuñécar hasn't been spared by the building craze. However, the town centre is still dominated by the characteristic white, cube-shaped houses

Phoenician *pickling pits* and the *Palacete La Najarra* in the *Av. de Europa* in neo-Arabic style. The *fortifications,* built by the Romans and extended by the Moors, are closed to visitors because they are unsafe. To make up for this, you can always climb the hill ⚜ *Peñón del Santo,* which offers a great view.

RESTAURANTS

Antonio
❖ Good fish dishes, really good value for money, well patronised by locals. *Bajos del Paseo Marítimo 12; Tel. 958 63 00 20; daily; category 2–3*

Bodega Francisco I
❖ Behind the tiled bar there is a confused jumble of barrels, on the wall hang hats and framed banknotes from every imaginable country under the sun, the television is always on, although the sound is turned off. The place, which bears

the first name of the original founder, has not changed one bit since it first opened its doors in 1951. *C. Real 15; Tel. 9586301 68; daily; category 2*

Horno de Candida
Good Andalusian cuisine. *C. Orovia 3; Tel. 958 63 4607; daily; category 2*

SHOPPING

In the historical town centre of Almuñécar, the shops are clustered around the Plaza de la Constitución, the sophisticated heart of the town, a very cosy, little square adorned with palm trees and more particularly on the Calle Real, a lengthy, winding shopping street. It is well worth doing more than window shopping here, because you can find almost everything that Marbella and Málaga have to offer, but at much more attractive prices. You can admire the latest fashions in the windows of the *Multicentro (Pl. de la Constitución 11)*. The speciality of the shop *Bordados (C. Vélez 1)* is to embroider a name, pictorial motif or any slogan requested by customers to any article of clothing within a few hours. Just opposite there is an old shop that stocks an amazing variety of straw hats, and nothing else. The *Calle Real* branches off from the other side of the Plaza. This is the place to go to find quality food stores.

ACCOMMODATION

Hotel Los Fenicios

Most of the 48 rooms have a view of the sea, the establishment is situated right beside the beach. *Paseo Marítimo Andrés Segovia s/n; Tel. 958 82 79 00; Fax 958 82 79 10; category 2*

Hotel Helios

The best hotel in town. *232 rooms; Paseo de San Cristóbal; Tel. 958 63 44 59; Fax 958 63 44 69; category 2–3*

Hotel Salobreña

Comfortable hotel with pool and tennis court, 6 km from the town in the direction of Salobreña. *192 rooms; N 340; Tel. 958 61 02 61; Fax 958 61 01 01; category 2–3*

Hostal Tropical

Very simple hostel, but close to the beach and inexpensive. *11 rooms; Av. de Europa s/n; Tel. 958 63 34 58; category 3*

INFORMATION

Oficina Municipal de Turismo

Palacete de la Najarra, Av. Europa s/n; Tel. 958 63 11 25; Fax 958 63 50 07; www.almunecar-ctropical.org

SURROUNDING AREA

La Herradura   (107 / E5)

The topography of this bay with a sea front promenade a few kilometres west from Almuñécar resembles a horseshoe. The little town has an inviting village-like plaza, covered in trees with pretty benches to sit on. For divers, there is the *Centro de Buceo (Paseo Marítimo 13; Tel. 958 64 06 57)*.

Salobreña   (107 / E5)

The most popular resort with the residents of Granada (pop. 9,000) is set on a rocky spur and consists of white, cube-shaped houses stacked up against one another, crowned by an Arab ⚐ fortress. From there, your gaze shifts to the Sierra Nevada. The oldest part of the town is a contorted maze of little alleys and stairways. The beach consists of coarse-grained sand, and here fisherman rent out rowing boats.

Accommodation: the *Pensión Marí Carmen* with its beautiful ⚐ terrace, is to be recommended *(14 rooms; C. Nueva 30; Tel. 958 610 906; category 3)*. The *Hotel Salambina*, is located a little outside Salobreña, and has 14 reasonably priced rooms with a fine view of the town. *(N 340; Tel. 958 61 00 37; Fax 958 61 13 28; category 3)*. The restaurant ⚐ ✪ *El Pesetos (C. Bóveda s/n; Tel. 958 61 01 82; closed Mon; category 2)* is a favourite amongst locals, the food is good and inexpensive. It also offers a view over the town and out to sea. The *El Peñón (Playa del Peñón; Tel. 958 61 05 38; daily; category 2)* stands on a rock in the sea and the food is divine.

The nerve centre of the South

The capital of the sun coast is far too beautiful for it to be no more than a transit station

The coastline is rugged, Africa lies just over the water, hot desert sand blows all around: the central section of the Costa del Sol, the most populated part of Andalusia, hardly possesses any of the natural attributes that would normally be ascribed to a paradise. The locals have managed to market the name of their coast on the world stage as being synonymous with *joie de vivre*, conjuring up images of near-heavenly pleasure. The lessons have been learned from the gigantic mistakes that were made in the boom period with its explosive growth in construction work, and the authorities have now got a firm grip on the helm as far as future developments are concerned.

ANTEQUERA

(106/B4) ★ Antequera (pop. 39,000) in the middle of fertile plain (*vega*) is more than a thousand years old and possesses two attractions: megalithic graves and a fantastic cliff maze. The town itself is worth a visit for its monumental

Mágala's promenade: the Paseo del Parque close to the harbour

architecture and the intimate squares in between. One such place is the Plaza de San Sebastián, which sets your heart racing just sitting on a stone bench or in a café. Just to think of the people who, over the centuries, have surveyed the hustle and bustle of the square from these balconies. It is one of those places that fines the imagination – suddenly, history ceases to be a school lesson as it comes alive before your eyes. It is just a shame that such heavy traffic swirls round the fountain and its pigeons. The many inclines in this town situated on several hills provide ample opportunity for you to boost your circulation – there are staircases and steep alleys everywhere. This means that the visitor is able to conquer step by step – in the literal sense of the word – one of the most beautiful towns in Spain.

SIGHTS

Historical Centre
The whole historical centre is under a preservation order. There are a large number of interesting religious and secular buildings. Two churches are particularly well

worth seeing: *Real Colegiata Santa María la Mayor (Pl. Santa María)*, a massive Renaissance building, and *El Carmen* on account of its pretty Artesonado roofs. Antequera possesses a total of 25 churches and monasteries, where nuns and monks still spend their days in seclusion. The *Arco de los Gigantis (C. de Pastillas)* is breathtakingly dignified. The Arch of Giants, a popular frame for photos, dates from 1585 and bears the coat of arms of the town of Antequera. Of the Moorish *fortifications*, only ruins remain. The site has been turned into a park, above which the angular clock tower ✹ *Torre de Papabellotas* dominates. From the vantage point of the top, you can get a view over the outlines of the buildings of Antequera. Your gaze will also turn towards the *Pena de Los Enamorados*, the hill of the lovers. The legend about this place is so typical of the Spanish taste for the dramatic. The daughter of rich Moors and her Christian lover were being pursued by henchmen, and so they threw themselves off the top of the hill, to be united forever in a shared death.

Cuevas

These prehistoric cave graves, which are considered to be one of the most significant relics of Iberian Megalithic culture and are located on the eastern edge of the town, are imbued with mystery. Nobody knows who constructed these graves and how they managed to transport the slabs of stone – some of which weigh 170 t – over the mountains. It is estimated that the site dates back to 2,500 BC.

The *Cueva de Menga* lies in a hill of slate and marl and the 25-m-long entrance to the burial chamber is bordered by five monoliths. The cave, which is 3.20 m high, is covered in limestone and is also supported by pillars. The total weight of the stones amounts to 1,600 t. There are mysterious drawings on one of the stones covering the wall. The *Cueva de Viera* was constructed using 27 wall stones that fitted together with great precision and is 19 m long. On top there is a single 4-m-long covering slab. The contents of the chamber were plundered after 1645, the year in which the caves were discovered. It is thought probable that both of these cave graves, which have been declared national monuments, were places where tribal leaders were buried, along with valuable artefacts. Four kilometres away, next to a sugar factory, is the *Romeral Cave*, whose origin has been dated at around 1800 BC. It is similar to the other two caves and the main chamber is in the form of a 4-m-high domed room. *Cueva de Menga and Cueva del Romeral: Tues and Thurs, 9 am–3.30 pm; Wed, Fri, Sat 9 am–6 pm; entry free; Cueva de Viera is closed for the time being for restoration*

RESTAURANTS

Parador de Antequera
The restaurant in the Parador is generally considered to be the best in town. *Paseo García del Olmo s/n; Tel. 952 84 02 6; daily; category 2*

La Rinconada
Andalusian cuisine in a beautiful arcade in the shade of a church. *C. San Agustín 1; Tel. 952 84 13 45; closed Sun; category 2*

SHOPPING

In the shopping thoroughfare *Duranes* there are a number of well-stocked fashion and shoe shops. *Rebajas* in the *Pl. de San Francisco 7* sells amusing pieces of jewellery and chains.

ACCOMMODATION

Colón
A maze-like establishment in the town centre. Not all of the 36 rooms have a bathroom. Large supermarket close by. *C. Infante Don Fernando 29; Tel./Fax 952 84 00 10; category 3*

Parador de Antequera
Mid-range hotel with a restaurant, swimming pool and beautiful garden. *55 rooms; Paseo García del Olmo s/n;Tel. 952 84 02 61; Fax 952 84 13 12, category 2*

La Yedra
Simple hotel in good location and good-value cafeteria. *22 rooms; N 331 km 136; Tel./Fax 952 84 22 87; category 2–3*

ENTERTAINMENT

❂ ♱ The young people of the town congregate in the *Cafetería Florida* at *C. Lucena 34* but also the kind of place where cake-devouring grandmothers don't feel out of place. Old-fashioned coffee house style, displays filled almost to bursting point, relaxed atmosphere.

INFORMATION

Oficina de Turismo
Pl. de San Sebastián 7; Tel./Fax 952 70 25 05

SURROUNDING AREA

El Torcal (106/B4)
In this nature park situated 16 km to the south, you can walk for several hours along marked routes though a labyrinth of huge blocks of limestone. This limestone plateau, covering an area of just under 20 sq km, with a height ranging from 1,000 to a good 1,300 m, has been eroded by the relentless attack of wind and water, leaving behind the most amazing cliff formations, particularly in those places where hard layers of limestone lie on top of softer ones. Nature

Marked paths lead through the weird sea cliffs at El Torcal

seems to have played some kind of game, leaving a surreal landscape on the reverse side of the Sierra Pelada, which enchants the visitor with its natural maze of passages, bridges, traverses and imploded craters. This background makes even more delightful the gentle country-house style of the *Posada del Torcal* in *Villanueva (10 rooms; Tel. 952 03 11 77; Fax 952 03 10 06; category 1–2).* Local delicacies are served on the terrace. Best of all is the majestic tranquility. Please note that travellers with children are not permitted to stay here.

FUENGIROLA

(**106/B6**) This former Roman Suel (pop. 43,000) is in fact of Phoenician origin. It is located right on the entrance to a tropical valley with sugar cane and sugar beet plantations in the shelter of the Sierra de Mijas, which acts as a natural wall. About the most attractive thing in this town, which has been suffocated under hideous blocks of concrete, is the promenade along the 6.5-km-long sandy beach, which has once again won the right to fly the blue EU flag. The liveliest part of Fuengirola is in fact on the water, especially off Puerto, where alongside the flashy, modern boats, fishing cutters also anchor. In summer, the swarms of visitors make their way along the ✪ ✳ Paseo Marítimo and through the historical quarter Casco Viejo.

SIGHTS

Castillo Sohail
✲ The castle on an overhang running out to the sea overlooking the mouth of the Río Fuengirola may be nothing more than a ruin today, but the imposing rectangular ground plan of the edifice can still be made out quite clearly. This fortification was built in 1730 on the site of a Moorish structure dating from the 10th century, which served over the centuries as a stronghold against piracy and was a strategic base. Before the Arabs, the Phoenicians and Romans had in turn built on this site. This place now forms the backdrop to summer music festivals and the presence of a *archeological museum* attests to its historical signifi-

cance. *Tues–Sun, 10 am–2.30 pm and 4 pm–6 pm, in Summer until 9 pm; 200 Ptas*

Casa del Bocadillo
✪ A snack bar with a wide range of sandwiches *(montados)*, which are freshly made. There are also salads on offer, but the locals tend to come here when they are in the mood for something more substantial. All dishes also to be taken away. *Av. Clemente Díaz; Tel. 952 46 96 40; closed evenings and Sun; category 3*

La Langosta
The oldest restaurant in the town specialises in lobster. It is always fresh. *C. Francisco Cano 1; Tel. 952 47 50 49; closed lunch time and Sun; category 1–2*

La Salina
Serrano ham dangles from the ceiling, *solomillo al escándalo* – finely chopped fillet of beef with roast potatoes and cream sauce – smells seductive. *Av. De Salina 26, Los Boliches; Tel. 952 47 18 06; closed Wed; category 2*

The *Mercadillo de los Martes* (every Tuesday) conjours up the atmosphere of the Orient amongst the dreary apartment blocks of Fuengirola. You are spoilt for choice when faced with the wide range of cards with meaningful and nonsensical mottoes to be found in the *Centro Comercial Las Rampas*. The *Juwelier Nicholson* stocks mainly silver jewellery in his boutique (*C. Marbella*).

Byblos Andaluz
Modern hotel with many comforts, situated in a tropical valley. Thalassotherapy/spa centre, two golf courses. *144 rooms; Urb. Mijas Golf; Tel. 952 46 02 50; Fax 952 47 67 83; category 1*

Camping Calazul
Located somewhat outside Fuengirola on the N 340, km 200, but reasonably priced, spacious and well equipped with supermarket and pool. *All year round; 300 places; Tel./Fax 952 49 32 19*

Florida
Well-kept, medium-sized establishment, prices won't make too big a dent in your wallet. *116 rooms; Paseo Marítimo s/n; Tel. 952 47 61 00; Fax 952 58 15 29, category 2–3*

Club Náutico de Fuengirola
Offers every kind of activity in and on the briny spray. *Tel. 952 47 04 06*

Palmeras Centre
Sport and leisure centre with many facilities, open all year round *Av. Martínez Catena; Tel. 952 46 16 48*

Parque Acuático Mijas
A relatively new leisure park in Mijas-Costa. A variety of swimming pools, several giant slides, roller coasters with sharp bends and steep drops. Particularly suited to families and offers a great many facilities for children. If your budget doesn't stretch to the prices in the restaurant, you can bring your own picnic. *Apr–June and Sept: daily*

*10 am–6 pm, July/Aug. 10 am–7 pm;
N 340 km 209; bus service from the
bus terminal in Fuengirola*

ENTERTAINMENT

There are exhibitions, concerts, plays and other performances at the culture centre ❂ *Casa de la Cultura (C. Estación Córdoba; Tel. 952 58 93 49)*. Every night *Fortuna Night Club* stages a big variety show with an international cast, and also Spanish ballet and flamenco. In addition, there is a casino *(daily 8.30 pm–4 am; from 3,500 Ptas)*. In the streets *Arroyo, Francisco Cano, Tejada* and *Vertedor* you will find *cinemas*, that never miss a Hollywood new release.

INFORMATION

Oficina de Turismo
Av. Jesús Santos Rein 6; Tel. 952 46 74 57; Fax 952 46 51 00

SURROUNDING AREA

Mijas   (106/A–B6)

★ ↘ 8 km away from Fuengirola lies one of the most attractive little towns (pop. 6,000) in the immediate inland area above the Costa del Sol, a town that resembles an amphitheatre in the way that it climbs up 430 m of a slope along a natural terrace. Mass tourism has been something of a mixed blessing for this "showcase of Andalusia". It is impossible to find even one peaceful little corner left in this town, forced to become a 24-hour open-air folklore museum. As long as you don't let a few things get on your nerves, like the not-too-pleasant fragrance of the donkeys of the *burro* taxis, and the pushy manner of the bow-legged drivers

of the said service, to say nothing of being ripped-off in the souvenir shops, you will still manage to discover in this village, founded around 2,600 years ago, a few morsels of the real Andalusia in the shape of cobbled alleys, wonderful balcony rails, decorative tiles, marble façades and many pine trees. The view of the villas and houses wedged in together on the slopes below Mijas is a dream come true.

You can get a good idea of how things once looked here from the *Plaza de la Constitución*, the *La Muralla Parish Church* with its Mudejar features and the *Casa Consistorial* (town hall), which also houses the *Tourist Office (Pl. Virgen de la Peña; Tel. 952 48 59 00)*. The *Carromato de Max*, a museum devoted to miniatures, has on display curiosities such as Leonardo da Vinci's *Last supper* on a grain of rice. The patron saint, La Virgen Santa María de la Pena, resides in a special ❂ *cave chapel* at the vantage point ↘ *Mirador de Mijas*. The rocky altar is overflowing with passport photos, pieces of cheap jewellery, hair bands and whole pieces of hair, even a few carefully shorn pigtails, with which people hope to win the favour of the saint. You can actually meet genuine *mijasueños* here, which is unusual, as this little town with its plesant highland climate is more than just a magnet that pulls in tourists daily by the busload, also most of the land is owned by foreigners. If you come on a Sunday during the bullfighting season, you can enquire about starting times and prices at the *Plaza de Toros* with its small arena, the only square one in Spain. Pride of place amongst the cheap shops goes to *Artesanías Granada (Pl. Virgen de la Peña s/n)* with beautiful vases, ceramics and

There is still the odd unspoilt corner to be found in Mijas

artistically embroidered bags. From mid-March until the end of September you can bet on the horse racing which takes place every Saturday at the racecourse, one of the largest in Europe covering an area of 1 million sq m. A large number of cafés and snack bars are temptingly lined up around the Plaza de la Constitución. For example, the ◀▶ *La Alcazaba (Pl. de la Constitución s/n; Tel. 952 59 02 53; closed Mon; category 2),* which serves international food and regional specialities such as lamb dishes. It also affords a view of the mountains and sea. The *El Capricho* is a rustic inn with a fine view of the centre of Mijas. *(C. Los Caños 5; Tel. 952 48 51 11; closed Wed; category 3).*

MÁLAGA

☛ City Map on pages 70/71

(106/B5) Gibralfaro castle high above Málaga is like a box seat in the theatre. The medieval citadel once served as a surveillance point for the whole coast. Today the watchers up in the exposed place no longer keep an anxious eye open for pirate ships. In their place, it is now freight ships that lie off the capital of the Costa del Sol. Evidence of explosive growth in the shape of cranes and the skeletons of new buildings loom up everywhere. During the Civil War in the thirties the much fought-over Málaga suffered repeated damage as a result of constant shelling and bombardment. Some 43 churches and monasteries were burnt down in 1931 alone, the year of the foundation of the Republic and by the time Málaga fell to the Fascists in 1937, the city centre was a wasteland. Commerce, harbour and tourism – these are the driving forces that Málaga has now succeeded in harnessing. The second largest city in Andalusia (pop. 535,000) also enjoys a healthy reputation amongst Spaniards as a good place to go shopping. Málaga is the nerve centre of the Spanish South. This city on the Río Guadalmedina, founded by the Phoenicians, transformed into a harbour town by the Romans, and adorned with masterpieces of architecture by the Arabs, is today synonymous with the economic revival of the Costa del Sol. Back in the 1980s this was still a rather rundown industrial and harbour town with a neglected city centre and a poor network of roads. A desire for reform was shared by property developers and the authorites, leading to the implementation in a short period of time of a programme of restoration and reconstrution which has far-reaching implications for the province as a whole. A no-nonsense approach meant that the programme to upgrade the centre was pushed through with militany precision. The result is that today in particular old squares and buildings like the Theater Miguel de Cervantes and the Plaza de la Merced have been given a new lease of life.

SIGHTS

Alcazaba (71/E2)

✅ The Moorish fortification dating from the 11th century on the castle hill was once the seat of the Nasrite rulers. Behind the concentric rings of walls, which were painstakingly restored in the 1930s, a maze of paths, little ornamental gardens with water jets, and lovely, round arches hidden. In the archaelogical exhibition rooms *(Mon–Sat, 10 am–1 pm and 5 pm–8 pm, Sun 10 am–2 pm, in winter 10 am–1 pm and 4 pm–7 pm; entry free)* some of the ceiling decorations are very beautiful.

Gibralfaro (71/F2)

✅ As you make the ascent up the hill by means of the rough, stone path which twists and turns in places, you gradually gain a better view of the city. By the time you reach the castle, you are rewarded with a superb view taking in a panorama of the harbour and sea, the town hall and bullfighting arena, historical buildings and the areas behind them which have been constructed more recently, the interlocking complex of highrises in the west and the villas and attractive residential areas in the south. With the aid of binoculars, you may even be able to make out toreros in the arena. Even without binoculars, it is clear that none of the high rises in Málaga is taller than the tower of the cathedral. *Get there on bus 35 from Paseo del Parque*

The Alazaba dominates Málaga and affords a splendid view of the town

Cathedral (71/D2)

The cathedral is nicknamed La Manquita, the one-armed, because it only has one tower and an unfinished stump the other. Thanks to a combination of lack of money and disputes over details that lasted for centuries, this Renaissance church was never completed. The construction based on plans by Diego de Siloé lasted 250 years (1528–1783). Its most striking features are the western and northern portals (the latter can be reached through the courtyard of oranges), and the most impressive thing about the interior is its majestic spaciousness (117 m long, 72 m wide). In the hall church with three aisles the vault is supported by mighty Corinthian pillars. Several grand masters of cathedral construction in the south of Spain worked on the church, including Alonso Cano. In spite of this, the western façade also remained uncompleted. *Daily 10 am–1 pm and 4 pm–5.30 pm; entry free; Pl. de la Catedral*

Paseo del Parque (71/D–F3)

✪ The *malagueños* are rightly proud of the promenade near to the harbour with its luscious, sub-tropical foliage. The park and paseo came in to being on the threshold of the 20th century as part of a comprehensive town planning programme, thanks to which lines of palm trees stand to attention for the benefit of resident and visitor alike. On public holidays whole families descend here, with the kids decked out in their Sunday finest. Old men and couples sit on the numerous benches and delight in the spectacle of the young people strolling by. If you decide to board one of the horse-drawn carriages, make sure that you agree on a price with the driver before you set off on the 20-to-30 minute trip.

Plaza de la Merced (71/E1–2)

★ ✪ ✶ The most beautiful square in the city has its fair share of pigeons fluttering about, a feature that was so important for the young Pablo Picasso. These feathered friends figure prominently in many of his pictures. The paved square-shaped area with its lovely old pavilions, with wrought-iron railings, is bordered by venerable, old houses which have now all been renovated. For as long as anyone can remember, this has been the place where people come to chat and flirt. Couples stroll hand in hand around the square, watched from balconies above by their more elderly fellow citizens.

Teatro Romano (71/E2)

A dispute raged for years: a palace on the Calle Alcazabilla was converted into a Casa de la Cultura and, in the process, walls dating back to the pre-Christain era were uncovered in the inner courtyard. Later, the terraces of an amphitheatre from the Roman era were discovered behind the house. The question was, should the Casa de la Cultura be torn down, thus allowing the Teatro Romano to be used for open-air theatrical performances? Both sides in this cultural war fought doggedly until finally in 1995 it was the house of culture that was sacrificed. The Roman theatre is to be excavated completely and a pedestrianised zone is to be created. It is an uplifting experience to walk around a site which, 2,000 years ago, was a forum for singers and orators alike to discuss the issues and problems of the day.

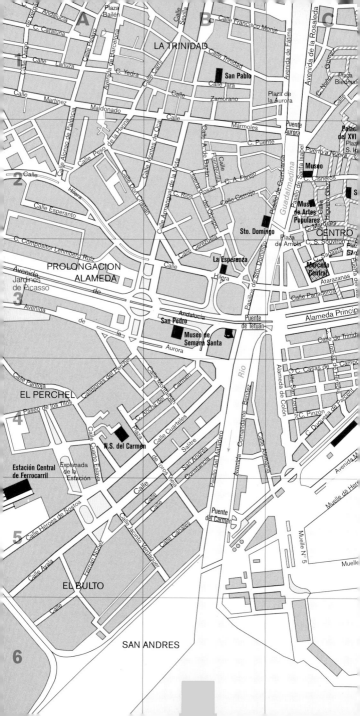

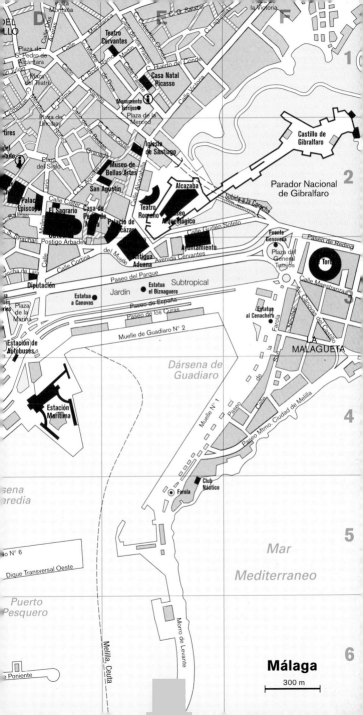

Málaga

300 m

MUSEUM

Casa Natal Pablo Picasso (71/E1)
A foundation set up at the end of the 1980s takes devoted care of the house in which the greatest son of the city was born. Pablo Picasso first saw the bright light of Málaga here on the 25th October, 1881. Thousands of books about the life and works of the painter, videos, posters and other objects – everything that has ever been said or written about Picasso, have been collected here. The rooms are full of documentation relating to stays here by the master. In the middle of things, art historians work away at their desks. In the Buenavista palace the former Museo de Bellas Artes is at present being converted into a Picasso museum. *Tues–Sat 10 am–1 pm and 5 pm–7 pm; 400 Ptas; Pl. de la Merced 15*

RESTAURANTS, BARS & CAFÉS

Antonio Martín (O)
✌ Traditional restaurant, opened in 1886, where you can sample the speciality of the town, the *fritura malagueña*, – with a view of the sea. *Paseo Marítimo 4, La Malagueta; Tel. 952 22 73 98; closed Sun; category 1–2*

Canadu
Vegetarian restaurant with a Picassoesque view of the Plaza de la Merced. Vitamin cocktails, Moroccan dishes, pasta and more. *Pl. de la Merced 21; Tel. 952 22 90 56; daily; category 2*

La Cancela (71/D2)
❖ This lively restaurant with rustic fittings and friendly atmosphere is very popular with the locals. Andalusian food, superb fish soups. *C. Denis Belgrano 3; Tel. 952 22 31 25; closed Wed; category 2*

El Chinitas (71/D2)
Wide-ranging selection of fish. In summer you dine out in the alley where the sound of live music echoes from the bars. *C. Moreno Monroy 4; Tel. 952 21 09 72; daily; category 3*

El Corte Inglés (70/B3)
❖ Large and inexpensive *buffet libre* in the cafeteria of the large department store. You can eat from the buffet to your heart's content, then pay at the cash desk on your way out. *Av. de Andalucía 4–6; closed Sun; category 2–3*

Gibralfaro (71/D2)
Pleasant cafeteria which has a good selection of tapas and sweets. *Pasaje Chinitas; closed Sun; category 3*

Lo Güeno (70/C3)
❖ ⚢ Polish off a snack and enjoy the great atmosphere. This is where the locals come to get into the mood for a night on the tiles. *C. Marín García 11; Tel. 952 22 30 48; daily; category 2*

El Jardín Cafetería (71/D2)
The fans rotate sluggishly, there is a note of class in the air, the piano with candle-holder and grandfather clock stand beneath the gold-framed mirror. In the summer months, the whole place gravitates outside onto the steps. *C. Canón 1; daily; category 2*

Orellana (71/D2)
❖ ⚢ Popular tapas bar well frequented by *malagueños*. *C. Moreno Monroy 3; Tel. 952 22 30 12; closed Wed; category 2–3*

Rincón del Trillo (70/C3)
The long, narrow bar on the ground floor is a place of pilgrim-

age for tapa aficionados. The restaurant on the top floor serves original fish dishes. *C. Esparteros 8; Tel. 952 22 31 35; closed Sun; category 2*

Café-Bar Santander (71/D2)
Basically furnished, but the tapas are excellent. *C. Granada 36; closed Sun; category 3*

La Tasca (70/C3)
❀ Small bar with an abundance of Serrano ham to nibble at between drinks. The bar is made of carved wood and you need a bit of patience as you try to fight your way through to it in the early afternoon and evenings. *C. Marín García 12; daily; category 3*

SHOPPING

Carrera (70/C2)
Jeans and young fashions in an unconventional shop where the music booms away. *C. Nueva 8*

Cosmopolis (71/D3)
A lot of delicacies: cheese, tinned fish, wine. *C. Marqués de Larios 2*

Galería de Arte (71/D2)
There is a new exhibition of work by Spanish artists every month in this old building in a central location. *C. Nino de Guevara 2*

Grabados Somera (71/D2)
In this tiny workshop in a small lane in the historical centre master Pedreo Somera Abad, the winner of many awards, produces artistic copperplates depicting folkloristic scenes, and also city views and animals. *C. Correo Viejo 7*

Mercado Central (70/C3)
Large covered market, run down, but full of fresh products from the Andalusian arable and livestock industries and fisheries. The central market in neo-Mudejar style has one interesting feature. The 14-m-high main entrance shaped like a horseshoe (13th century) is adorned with two coats of arms and the inscription "Only Allah is the victor". *Mon–Sat, 8 am–3 pm; C. Atarazanas 8*

Collector's market (71/D2)
Stamps, old coins and banknotes as well as pictures and photographs, particularly postcards. A treasure trove for numismatists. *Sun mornings; Pl. de la Constitución*

Zara (70/C3)
Boutique in the pedestrianised zone with everything that young, Mediterranean people find chic. You can usually find a few bargains here. *C. Liborio García 6*

ACCOMMODATION

Don Curro (71/D3)
Three-star hotel on the edge of the city centre, good base for fans of a stroll. *118 rooms; C. Sancha de Lara 7–9; Tel. 952 22 72 00; Fax 952 21 59 46; category 2*

Youth hostel
(Albergue de la Juventud) (O)
If you have a youth hostel identity card, you can stay here very cheaply in a four-bed room. *Pl. Pio XII 6 (last stop on bus route 18); Tel. 952 30 85 00; Fax 952 30 85 04; category 3*

Larios (71/D3)
Hyped-up atmosphere, 40 cool rooms, historical façade – in the middle of the town. *C. Marqués de Larios 2; Tel. 952 22 22 00; Fax 952 22 24 07; category 1–2*

Las Vegas (O)

Practical hotel on the edge of the city, with 34 new rooms in the extension overlooking the sea. *106 rooms; Paseo de Sancha 22; Tel. 952 21 77 12; Fax 952 22 48 89; category 2*

Málaga Palacio (71/D3)

꙰ The best establishment in Málaga despite the high-rise architecture. Boasts a swimming pool on the roof terrace and a wonderful view. *225 rooms; Cortina del Muelle 1; Tel. 952 21 51 85; Fax 95 22 25 10 03; category 1*

Los Naranjos (O)

Hotel in Andalusian style with underground garage on the edge of the town centre. *41 rooms; Paseo de Sancha 35; Tel. 952 22 43 16; Fax 952 22 59 75; category 2*

Parador de Málaga Gibralfaro (71/F2)

꙰ This hotel, which was renovated and reopened in 1995, is situated by the Moorish fortifications. Romantics will love watching sunrises and the light playing on the sea at dusk from the terrace or the swimming pool. There is a golf course close by with a golf and tennis school. *38 rooms; Pl. de Gibralfaro 1; Tel. 952 22 19 02; Fax 952 22 19 04; category 1*

Parador de Málaga del Golf (O)

Tucked into a golf course in Churriana to the south west. Traditional Andalusian style. *60 rooms; Autovía E 15, Exit Parador/Aeropuerto; Tel. 952 38 12 55; Fax 952 38 89 63; category 1*

Sur (70/C3)

Really good-value hotel in prime loation, peacefully set in a pedestrianised zone behind the Alameda Principal. *37 rooms; C. Trinidad Grund 13; Tel. 952 22 48 03; Fax 952 21 24 16; category 3*

SPORTS & EXCURSIONS

Lauro Golf Los Caracolillos (Alhaurín de la Torre; Tel. 952 41 27 67) is an 18-hole golf course in an attractive setting. You can get information about golf courses in the whole province from *Federación de Golf de Andalucía (Paseo del Pintor Sorolla 34; Tel. 952 22 55 90).* Riding school and equestrian performances at *Centro Ecuestre Arteeus (Apartado 94, Alhaurín de la Torre; Tel. 952 41 28 18).* Information for sailing enthusiasts from *Club Náutico El Candado (Playa Almellones, El Palo; Tel. 952 29 60 97).* Within the city limits of Málaga there are more than 15 beaches (*Pedregalejo, El Palo* and ✪ *La Malagueta* are particularly attractive).

SPANISH COURSES

Especially for young people, taking part in a Spanish course is ideal for those who wish to get to know Spain as well as learn Spanish. The *Malaca Instituto* and its school premises *Club Hispánico,* where accommodation is also offered (double rooms) is situated on a hill 15 minutes by bus from the centre of Málaga. (*Cerrado de Calderón, C. Cortada 6, 29018 Málaga; Tel. 952 29 32 42; Fax 952 29 63 16).* The average age is lowest on the summer holiday courses, at 16 to 25. The great variety of courses on offer, ranging from the standard course of 20 hours per week to six hours' individual tuition per day, means that it is possible to accommodate older participants. Recently, courses for the top end of the age scale have been offered. This does much more than just teach you how to roll the r in "gracias", with the additional option of taking courses in flamenco dancing, aerobics and massage, whilst a cookery course will help you to acquire the knack of making typical local meals. The price for two weeks with half board is in the region of 100,000 to 175,000 Ptas.

ENTERTAINMENT

Antigua Casa de Guardia (70/C3)
A wine store opened in 1840, where more than 20 red wines can be tasted from the barrels which fill a large part of the room. You stand at the counter and at little tables, have your glass filled and wash it down with a morsel of seafood. *Two entrances; Alameda Principal 18 and C. Pastora 6*

Calle Beatas (71/D2)
◉ ☆ This alley, which branches off from the Calle Granada, seems to exert a magical power over young locals. Particularly at weekends, things get pretty wild in the bars and pubs. It doesn't matter how shy you are, you can't help making the acquaintance of *malagueños* here.

El Pimpi (71/D2)
◉ ☆ One of the most original pubs. Artists and young people set the pace. Pimpi, consisting of a number of rooms leading from one to the next and ivy-clad ceilings, is really spacious. *C. Granada 62*

Salsa (71/D1–2)
☆ Pub where the programme for the whole evening, as the name would suggest, is devoted to nothing other than *música salsa*. Amazing atmosphere. *C. Méndez Núñez 1*

Teatro Cervantes (71/D1)
Opera, dance and music festivals, also avant-garde theatre in the classified building, a palace restored in 1987. *Pl. del Teatro, Information: Tel. 952 22 02 37; bookings: Tel. 952 22 41 00; tickets 1,500 to 2,500 Ptas*

INFORMATION

Oficina de Turismo (71/D2)
Pasaje de Chinitas 4 (close to the Pl. de la Constitución); Tel. 952 21 34 45; Fax 952 22 94 21

SURROUNDING AREA

Jardín Botánico-Histórico de la Concepción (106/B5)
◉ Sprawling botanic garden with tropical and subtropical flora interspersed with some archeological finds from the region. The guided tour lasts an hour and in summer, buses run on Sat and Sun from the Alameda Principal to the park, a great favourite with families. *Tues–Sun 10 am–5.30 pm, in summer until 8 pm; entry free; N 331 km 166*

Bird watching park El Retiro (106/B5)
This finca in Churriana, established in 1669, 10 km south west of Málaga, has recently been reopened following renovation. Directed by a German ornithologist, the park, with its many trees, bird houses and little waterfalls, had become the home of thousands of species from five continents. *Daily 9 am–6 pm; take the N 340; admission 1,250 Ptas, children 600 Ptas*

NERJA

(107/D5) ★ This is one place where the authorities weren't caught napping. No get-rich-quick developers were permitted to stick up monstrosities disguised as hotels in this pretty little town (pop. 14,000). On the contrary, the hotels are small, the atmosphere is relaxed, almost intimate. In short, Nerja has managed to preserve its antiquated charm. Even the beaches can be a good place to get some peace and quiet since each one occupies its own picturesque little bay seperated by cliffs. They are all joined by a footpath that snakes its way below the town, where the *carabineros* once marched up and down on patrol. The beaches and water are very clean. For the price of 350 Ptas you can take a trip on the miniature railway that rattle through Nerja every 30 minutes, departing from in front of the Hotel Ríu Mónica.

SIGHTS

Balcón de Europa

◁▷ ✿ The view afforded from here is second to none. This amazing palm-lined, flower-filled promenade on a massive cliff stretches well out into the sea between two delightful bays. The great concentration of cafés and restaurants in this area, means that it is a magnet for the locals. The last vestiges of a fortress and two iron cannon act as reminders of the past.

Cuevas de Nerja

The stalactite caves immediately outside Nerja, formed due to the precipitation of calcium carbonate, span some 800 m in length and 60 m in height. The cave paintings with dolphin motifs are thought to be 20,000 years old. Amazing stalactities hang in the chamber-like caves. Visitors are especially enchanted by the magical light and the unique sound effects. The good acoustics are also commercially exploited – in July, nightly concerts and ballet performances are held in front of this ancient backdrop. The performances take place in the so-called Chamber of Cascades in the caves, where the stalactites and stalagmites give the stage its inimitable appearance. Potholers have recently discovered the delights of venturing down in small groups to the *galerías altas*, previously the sole preserve of scientists because it is none too easy to access. (Information: *Patronato de la Cueva de Nerja, Ctra. de Maro s/n; Tel. 952 52 95 20; Fax 952 25 96 46; www.bd-andalucia.es/ cuevanerja.html).* The caves, with more than half a million visitors annually, have become the second most popular tourist attration in Andalusia after the Alhambra. *May–mid–Sept. Mon–Sat 10 am– 2 pm and 4 pm–6.30 pm, Sun 10 am– 2.30 pm and 4 pm–7 pm; admission: 665 Ptas, children 300 Ptas*

RESTAURANTS

There is something to suit every pocket and every taste. For those in search of a bit of class, there is the *Casa Luque (Pl. Cavana 2; Tel. 952 52 10 04; closed Mon; category 1–2),* where fine food is served in a subtropical garden beneath palm trees. If you are looking for something a bit cheaper, try the *Los Sevillanos (C. Chapari s/n, Edificio Corona; Tel. 952 52 56 06; closed Wed; category 2)* and *Benítez* right next to the sea *(C.*

The caves of Nerja are home to the most unusual concert hall in Spain

Carabeo 50; Tel. 952 52 22 08; daily; category 2), for Andalusian cuisine.

The idea of sampling German food whilst in Spain may seem rather odd, but in fact the German *Udo Heimer* is one of the best cooks on the Costa del Sol. He has received many awards from the Spanish Gastronomic Association for delights such as "piquant goulash soup Hamburg" and "beef olive with cabbage", and he has also received "The Golden Cook Medal for World Best Restaurants" from the USA. Reservation essential *(Pueblo Andaluz 27; Tel. 952 52 00 32; closed Wed; category 1).*

A totally different experience is offered by the restaurant ◀▷ *Cueva de Nerja* directly opposite the entrance to the caves. Everyday between the hours of midday and 4 pm the *Gran Buffet Libre* is on offer, allowing everyone to eat as much as they like for a set price of 1,250 Ptas. Children up to the age of three eat for nothing, and up to the age of seven they pay half price.

The largest open buffet on the Sun Coast is groaning with tasty surprises, and the view of the sea is thrown in for free.

SHOPPING

The junk shop *Carmari (C. Pintada 34)* with its pink façade, thick fabrics and knick-knacks is out of this world. The *Casa del Arte (C. Cristo 13)* deals in artistic handicrafts and oil paintings with motifs from the Andalusian region. Angela Minguez serves in her own shop *Gaia (C. Cristo 18)* and is only too happy to tell visitors in Spanish or English, backed up by gestures, how she produces her glassware. There are also dresses, bags, jewellery – all hand made.

ACCOMMODATION

Paraíso del Mar

Privately-run, well-kept little hotel next to the Parador in Nerja, overlooking the sea. *18 rooms; C. Prolon-*

gación de Carabeo 22; Tel. 952 52 16 21; Fax 952 52 23 09; category 2

Perla Marina

New hotel with its own beach. Lovely restaurant terrace. *107 rooms; C. Mérida 7; Tel. 952 52 33 50; Fax 952 52 40 83; category 2*

Ríu Mónica

Newly-opened establishment at the Playa de Torrecilla. The swimming pool is heated in winter. Also children's pool, sun terrace, subtropical park, tennis court, activities for children. *234 rooms; Playa de Torrecilla; Tel. 952 52 11 00; Fax 952 52 11 62; category 1*

SPORT, BEACHES & OUTINGS

Tourists have recently been granted access to the municipal multi-sport complex. There are facilities, amongst others, for a variety of ball games including tennis and badminton.

For those with a taste for nude bathing, there are a number of relatively inaccessible parts of the beach (steep descents) between Nerja and Almuñécar where this pleasure has been legalised. It is up to you to decide which one is the bay of your dreams.

At the tourist office you can get a free brochure prepared by the municipality which contains a lot of very useful information for those with a love of walking, and especially for those who want to get to know the coastal area with its many bays. There is, for example, a three and a half hour walk from the Balcón de Europa to the Cuevas de Nerja. It takes two and a half hours to get to Punta Lara, and four and a half hours to the Castillo Alto.

Viajes Altasierra (C. Los Huertos 1; Tel. 952 52 74 10; Fax 952 52 66 39) offers jeep safaris to the nature reserves at Sierra de Almijara and Sierra Tejeda. The four-wheel drive cars can be rented with a driver or on their own. The price of 6,950 Ptas (children aged under 12, 5,950 Ptas) includes a barbecue in a country house in the mountains. A down-to-earth excursion.

ENTERTAINMENT

This little town boasts a truly great nightlife. To get into the mood, you avail yourself of the happy hour starting at 8 pm in the *Jardín Dada (Prolongación Antonio Millón),* make an appearance at the *Pub Coconuts (C. Pintada 11)* which doesn't open until 10 pm, and after midnight you move along a few doors down to the ✪ ✵ *Bar 23 Bar (C. Pintada 23),* which always attracts a good crowd and for the benefit of non-smokers has a little inner courtyard where they can get a few breaths of fresh air.

INFORMATION

Oficina de Turismo

Puerta del Mar 2; Tel. 952 52 15 31; Fax 952 52 62 87

SURROUNDING AREA

Frigiliana   (107/D5)

For 6 km, you endure the tortuous curves of the Ruta del Sol y del Vino, which is swallowed up by mountains above Nerja, before finally reaching the most beautiful village in Spain. It has been voted such many times, and even the King has been here. Stairways twist and turn, geraniums are in bloom, donkeys still carry loads, old women sweep the paving stones. A veritable, *pueblo blanco* straight out of the guide books. *Nekane (C. San Sebastián 30; Tel. 952 53 33 82; closed Sun lunchtime and Sat; category 2–3)* goes in for satisfying plain fare, served in an inner courtyard adorned with flowers. Guests staying at the ❧ hotel *Las Chinas (9 rooms; Pl. Capitán Cortés 14; Tel./Fax 952 53 30 73; category 3)* are treated to a great view of the countryside.

Torre del Mar / Vélez-Málaga (106/C5)

Torre del Mar, which lies to the west of Nerja, is in fact the coastal zone of the town of Vélez-Málaga (pop. 54,000), which is situated slightly inland. The old Phoenician settlement on a hill in the fertile valley of the river possesses a remarkably intact historical core with a maze of alleys and original buildings. The most notable are the splendid *Palacio de los Marqueses de Beniel* dating from the 17th century, the *Santa María la Mayor* church with its three aisles, which has preserved its Mudejar style, and the *Fernandos VI* fountain dating from the 18th century. Towering up over everything are the imposing watchtowers of the Moorish fortifications, of which but a few walls remain standing.

Torre del Mar is a typical *urbanización,* practical, but lacking in character. The long beach with its coarse-grained sand is not particularly well eqiupped, but the amount of space provided goes a long way to compensate for this. As of 2000 Vélez is trying to make a name for itself as a "Costa del Amor". To this end, the municipality is switching off the beach lighting at one in the morning for one hour at the beaches of Caleta de

Véley and Torre del Mar. There is a reasonable camping site at: *Caravaning Laguna Playa; 160 places; turn off the N340 after the built-up area and follow the signs; Tel. 952 54 06 31; Fax 952 54 04 84*

TORREMOLINOS

(106/B5–6) Some 90 pubs, 40 discos, 80 fish restaurants and numerous night bars: Torremolinos (pop. 28,000) is no treasure trove of Andalusian folklore; it is a machine geared to the requirements of international tourism. This place, with its fine sandy beach and many beach bars and sports facilities, has plenty to offer those in search of relaxation rather than culture, although it must be said that this huge *urbanización* is an ideal departure point for interesting excursions of a more cerebral nature. The most significant resort in the middle of the Costa del Sol was, up until a few decades ago, an insignificant little fishing hamlet with 15 houses. Its career began a few kilometres further west in Montemar, where in 1932 the visionary and business-minded Carlotta Alessandri acquired a plot of mountainous land. When she was asked what kind of plants she planned to grow on this unfruitful land, the courageous lady retorted "tourists" and spoke with enthusiasm of the "Spanish Riviera".

It was after the World War II that the socialite Marqués de Nájera built a residence in Torremolinos, and he was followed by well-to-do families, as well as curious aristocrats and eccentrics of all kinds to the permanent sunshine. It wasn't long before the world of the arts was sending its own representatives, particularly film stars and writers. Torremolinos – "Tower of the Windmills" – and there are still a few windmills left in the quarter of Pimentel – had become the playground of hedonists, and later of all kinds of never-do-wells.

San Miguel

The quarter of the town, with the pedestrian precinct of the same name, the *Plaza Costa del Sol* and the neighbouring streets, forms the fashionable centre. The sea end of the long Calle San Miguel ends at a *Moorish tower* dating from the 14th century. The Cuesta del Tajo takes you to the *Molino la Bóveda*, a windmill from the 16th century, and from there on to the *Playa Bajondillo*, which is separated by a rocky head from the equally popular *Playa Carihuela*.

RESTAURANTS

La Chacha

Unpretentious restaurant recommended for its concoctions using freshly caught fish. *Av. Palma de Mallorca s/n; Tel. 952 38 49 10; closed Tues; category 3*

Mesón Galego Antoxo

Galician cuisine in a stylish town-centre restaurant with a large garden section. *C. Hoyo 5; Tel. 952 38 45 33; closed Sun evening; category 2*

Beach restaurants

The restaurants listed below *(all category 2–3)* at the Playa Carihuela, the sea front promenade of the old fishing village, (entry via the street branching off at the Hotel Las Palomas) are all to be recommended, as they are dedicated to the traditional art of cooking seafood without any unnecessary frills. Why not sample *pescaíto frito*, the little fish fried in olive oil, which is cooked to prefection in these parts. The best thing to accompany it is a cool sherry. *Guaquín, C. Carmen 37; Tel. 952 38 45 30; El Roqueo, C. Carmen 35; Tel. 952 38 49 46; La Jábega, C. Mar 17, Tel. 952 38 63 75; La Marina, Paseo Marítimo 23; Tel. 952 38 93 71*

SHOPPING

You could stroll away a whole day in the pedestrianised street *Calle San Miguel* just window shopping or maybe stopping to buy something, eating ice cream, drinking coffee and simply looking. Alongside the unavoidable souvenir shops, ambitious fashion and jewellery stores have been opened. Fresh produce is on sale every Thursday at the food market beside the Town Hall. The finest and most expensive goods are on sale at the jewellery and clock store *Ideal (C. San Miguel 38)*, and if you have met the treasure of your life on the beach, what better way to mark this event than by engraving the name of your lover on your person? There is a professional tattooing service at *Templo Tattoos (Pl. de Gamba Alegre)*.

ACCOMMODATION

Beatriz

Small *hostal* on the beach. The view from the balcony streches to the Playa de Bajondillo. *8 rooms; C. Peligros 4; Tel. 952 38 51 10; category 3*

Guadalupe

Hostal with sea view, a few rooms have balconies. Good-value in-house restaurant. *8 rooms; C. Peligros 15; Tel. 952 38 19 37; category 3*

Meliá Costa del Sol

Large hotel on the seashore; theoretically there is no need to leave the premises, where there are several restaurants, shops and entertainment. 555 rooms, almost two thirds of which have a sea view. *Paseo Marítimo 19; Tel. 952 38 66 77; Fax 952 38 64 17; category 1–2*

Pez Espada

Traditional establishment on the Playa de Carihuela with tropical garden, two pools, fitness centre and sauna. *205 rooms; Av. Salvador Allende 11; Tel. 952 38 03 00; Fax 952 37 28 01; category 2*

Sol Don Pedro

Peaceful hotel close to the beach with children's playground, pools, tennis, bowling and sherry bar. *295 rooms; Av. Del Lido s/n; Tel. 952 38 68 44; Fax 952 38 69 53; category 2*

SPORTS & LEISURE

The largest water pleasure park on the Sun Coast – wild slides, trained dolphins – is to be found here in the shape of *Atlantis Aquapark* near the Palacio de Congresos *(Ctra. de Circunvalación s/n; Mid-May–Sept, daily 10am–8pm; admission: 2,000 Ptas, children 1,500 Ptas).* There are reserved sections for surfers on all beaches. Motorbikes can be rented at *Autos Alba (Av. Carlotta Alessandri; Tel. 952 37 41 37).*

ENTERTAINMENT

The majority of the ✥ discotheques are situated around the central Plaza Costa del Sol. Things don't really get going much before mid-

night and in summer there is no let-up until the next day begins to dawn. The disco *Eugeno's (C. Casablanca 14)* has dance floors on two levels, the *Palladium (Av. Palma de Mallorca 36–38)* even has a pool.

INFORMATION

Oficina de Turismo

Pl. de Blas Infante 1; Tel. 952 37 95 11; Fax 952 37 95 51; www.spa.es/torremolinos

SURROUNDING AREA

Alhaurín el Grande   (106/A5)

This picturesque village is a mere 20 km island from the hubbum of the resort – but this is a different world entirely. It nestles on the edge of the Sierra de Mijas, the very epitome of peace and tranquility. In addition to the *ruins of the fortress* from the Moorissh era, the *Ermita de la Virgen de la Pena* is situated in a cave next to the *parish church.* A more recent attraction appeals to the youngest visitors: the first 18-hole children's golf course in the world. A round at the *Alhaurín Golf & Country Club* costs 1, 800 Ptas.

Cable car in Benalmádena   (106/B6)

⟡ A recent new attraction is the 8-km-long cable car route leading from the base station Arroyo de la Miel to the peak of Mount Calamorro. Covering a length of over 600 m, it also crosses over the Tívoli amusement park. When skies are clear, from the mountain peak you can see the whole of the Costa del Sol and right across to the Moroccan coast. *Daily 10 am–8 pm; in summer until midnight; 900 Ptas.*

The old favourite makes a comeback

Varied experiences from elite Mediterranean tourism to the unspoilt hinterland

This one-time playground of high society and concrete jungle is now inexorably metamorphosing into a string of towns with Andalusian charm. This process of change has taken root throughout the western Costa del Sol. This area is blessed with a microclimate guaranteeing an average of 320 days of sun per year. Although you would be hard put to find the same concentration of luxury hotels anywhere else, and no coastal strip anywhere in Europe boasts such a large number of golf courses, this picturesque stretch of land is no longer the sole preserve of those who ostentatiously flash their wealth with powerful limousines and other cuirs and graces. The idle beach existence of the international jet set is no longer a free spectacle to be observed on the beaches and promenades, it has long since migrated to the ghettoes of the club grounds and to private estates. The demise of this gaudy pageant put on for the benefit of the paparazzi has opened the way for tourists genuinely seeking new experiences. Visitors to the

The most luxurious yachts of all are still to be seen in and around Marbella

Costa del Sol are today witnessing the comeback of this old favourite, more brilliant than ever before.

ESTEPONA

(**11/E-F3**) Not quite in the same class as Marbella, but it makes up for this in originality. Tiled roofs, balconies strewn with flowers, street names on ceramic tiles. Estepona (pop. 31,000) feels at ease with the world. Moorish and Christian culture have produced a most agreeable cocktail here, reflected both in the architecture and in the atmosphere. The beaches are up to 40 m wide and the palm trees lend a South Seas atmosphere. A beach police force with 80 officers keep an eye on the proceedings. The sea front promenade was lengthened in 1998.

SIGHTS

Historical centre
The centre of the town, with its maze of alleys and elaborate houses, is typically Andalusian. The *parish church* was built in the 15th century. In the *C. Castillo* you can still see remains of the *town wall* built by the Moors. The place

MARCO POLO SELECTION: MARBELLA AND THE WEST

1 Plaza de los Naranjos in Marbella
Square of the Orange Trees: where local and visiting strollers rub shoulders (page 87)

2 Casares
This mountain village was fought over for centuries and has a special atmosphere and great views (page 85)

where residents and visitors to the town congregate and meet up is the ✪ ☨ *Plaza de las Flores,* chock-a-block on warm days with café chairs and the place where all the young people hang out.

RESTAURANTS & BARS

Da' Medici
Refined Italian cuisine set off against a sumptuous décor. The very best in salads and pasta. *Urb. El Pilar; Tel. 952 88 46 87; closed lunch time and Sun; category 1–2*

Río Verde
Great little place with a knack for creating light delicacies out of local fish produce at prices that don't stretch the budget. *Av. Juan de Chinchilla; Tel. 952 86 64 61; closed Sun; category 2–3*

Los Rosales
◁◿ Good and inexpensive tapa bar with a great variety of seafood creations. *C. Damas 12; category 3*

SHOPPING

Flea market
Every *Sun, 9 am–3 pm* in *Puerto Estepona:* jewellery, antiques, leather goods, artistic handicrafts.

Maduarte Decoración
If you are looking for that extra little something to complete the decoration of your home, a trip to this shop situated in particularly attractive premises should pay dividends. *Pl. Fernando Sánchez Dragó 1*

ACCOMMODATION

Buenavista
Simple establishment, but in a good location. *38 rooms; Paseo Marítimo 180; Tel. 952 80 01 37; Fax 952 80 55 93: category 3*

Las Dunas Beach
A luxury hotel in Andalusian style directly on the beach. *175 rooms; Ctra. de Cádiz km 163.5; Tel. 952 79 43 45; Fax 952 79 48 25; www.las-dunas.com, category 1*

Kempinski
Luxury resort hotel covering 60,000 sq m with sub-tropical gardens, waterfalls, palms and a beach. Opened in 1999, the architectural style is Moorish and the internal furnishings are modern. 250 rooms, more than 100 of which are suites. Several restaurants and bars, business centre, wellness centre, fitness world, heated swimming pools inside and out, sauna, Turk-

ish baths, beauty salon, tennis courts, special arrangements with 30 golf clubs in the vicinity – in short, an unbeatable hotel. *Ctra. de Cádiz km 159; Tel. 952 80 95 00; Fax 952 80 95 50; category 1*

BEACHES & HEALTH FACILITIES

Naturism

3 km inland from Estepona all is bared. The facilities at the nudist village Costa Natura include a number of swimming pools, playing fields, holiday homes and shops. *Urb. Costa Natura, N 340 km 151; Tel. 952 80 80 65; Fax 952 80 80 74; www.costanatura.com*

Health Centre

At the *Centro de Medicina Tradicional China,* which is attached to the Hotel El Paraíso, the bodies of patients receive the attention of oriental masseuses and slimming, anti-smoking and anti-stress programmes are carried out under medical supervision. *N 340 km 167, Tel. 952 88 30 00; Fax 952 88 20 19*

INFORMATION

Oficina de Turismo

Paseo Marítimo Pedro Manrique s/n; Tel. 952 80 09 13; Fax 952 79 21 81

SURROUNDING AREA

Casares **(111/E3)**

★ You won't find anything more spectacular than the wild and romantic Sierra Bermeja inland of Estepona. Casares, situated on a 440-m-high plateau, swings into sight out of the blue as you drive through the wooded, mountainous landscape. A collection of white houses look as if they have been scattered at random up the mountain, watched over by an Arab fortress. All the Muslim princes coveted this little town with the result that Casares was fought over for centuries until, in the 15th century, the Christians marched in. You roam through the sloping alleys, climb up narrow, well-trodden staircases and enter the *San Sebastián* church dating from the 17th century with its statue of the Virgen del Rosario del Campo. A survey has revealed that not a single inhabitant of this *pueblo blanco* has the least desire to move away. The population has remained constant for the past 200 years: approximately 3,000 souls reside here. The higher up you go, the more stunning the view. From above, the non-too-distant Mediterranean glistens beyond the olive groves, vegetable gardens and woods.

This little town on a saddle – the only possible transit point between two mountain ranges – was in an ideal location from which to control the roads. Not so much a military question as one of finance. The Phoenicians were the first to exact road tolls, and all their successors followed suit. Now nobody keeps watch from the ruined fortress in search of victims to be forced to dig deep into their pockets. The alleys of this town, which seems to have been modelled on an ants' nest, are tiny and the fountain in the middle adds to the romance of the place. The finest thing is not Casares itself, but the views out over the surrounding countryside. The goats' cheese in olive oil is said to be the best local produce. You can sample it in the small eateries such as *Curro (C. Barriada los Ponis; Tel. 952 89 52 05; closed Sun; category 3)* or in *La Terraza*

(Ctra. Local; Tel. 952 89 40 40; closed Sun; category 2). To honour the progressive politician Blas Infante, who aroused Andalusia from its archaic backwardness in the first half of the 20th century and was murdered by Franco's soldiers, a small *museum* carrying his name has been opened – *(C. Carrera 51; Tues–Sat 10 am–1 pm).* If you wish to spend more time here, ask for a room at the simple, centrally located *Hostal Plaza (9 rooms; Pl. de España; Tel. 952 89 40 88; category 3).*

San Roque (111/E4)

This white town above the Bay of Algeciras is the place where the road to Gibraltar forks off. Just on the border with the British Crown Colony is one of the jewels in the Andalusian culinary crown. Alejandro Gavilán, chef at the restaurant *Los Remos (Finca Villa Victoria; Tel. 956 69 84 12; closed Sun; category 2),* is one of the stars in this department. Dining here is like an act of worship in a stucco shrine. The seven-course gourmet dinner costs only 6,000 Ptas in spite of its high quality. There can hardly be another establishment where fish receives the same ambitious treatment. You only have yourself to blame if you don't stop off on your way to Gibraltar!

Tarifa (111/D5)

A must for surfers, where it never stops blowing. The southernmost tip of Europe is never free of wind – which is just what the acrobats mounted on their boards need to be able to ride the waves at speeds of almost 40mph. This is the meeting point of two powerful wind systems: the Levante rages from the east through the 10-km-

long bay and the Poniente gusts from the west at the end of the bay, where most of the surfers congregate. Beginners and those at more advanced levels can take lessons from 3,500 Ptas per hour. You can dine at reasonable prices in the restaurant *La Nueva Urta (Pl. Juan de Austria; Tel. 956 68 06 69; daily; category 3),* and stay at the *Hurricane Hotel (33 rooms; N 340 km 78; Tel. 956 68 49 19; Fax 956 68 03 29; category 1-2),* surrounded by a subtropical garden, or at a simple hotel in the town centre *La Mirada (25 rooms; C. San Sebastián 48; Tel. 956 68 44 27; Fax 956 68 11 62; category 3).* The in place to be at night is the ✱ Bar *La Ruina (C. Santa Trinidad 9)* on the town wall. If you would like to see whales and dolphins, there are excursions led by the skippers of *firmm España* out into the Straits of Gibraltar *(Departure point: Pedro Cortés 3, near Café Central; Tel. 956 62 70 08; 4500, 3000 Ptas). Information: Patronato local de Turismo, Paseo de la Alameda; Tel./Fax 956 68 09 93*

MARBELLA

(106/A6, 111/F3) Marbella (pop. 84,000) has two faces: on the one hand it is a glitzy town of glass, concrete and glamour, which has made such a name for itself as a centre for elite and jet set tourism, but in the background is the old heart of the town, leading a kind of parallel existence. You can only claim to know Marbella if you have seen and experienced both. You should sit in the Plaza de los Naranjos in the evening, when the square is bathed in the ivory light of the candelabras. This has been the centre point of the town for centuries. At the same time as the rich and beautiful are strolling along the sea front promenade, which is said to have cost 127,500 Ptas per metre, between the quays where the yachts are bobbing up and down, the young people of Marbella are meeting up in the Square of the Orange Trees. This is also where old people come to chat, couples look in the boutiques, and children run noisily around the alleys.

SIGHTS

Historical centre

The oldest quarter of the town lies on the hill some distance from the sea. With its narrow alleys where dogs doze on the doorsteps of old houses, it is a photogenic mixture of Moorish and Christian styles. The *Rincón de la Virgen* at the junction of the two streets Remedios and Dolores is adorned with wildly colourful bougainvillea. The Rococo gates of the Church of Incarnation *(Iglesia Mayor de la Encarnación)* dating from the 16th century, at the end of the Calle de Carmen, open into a romantic, little church square, over-shadowed by the tower of a once splendid Moorish palace dating from the 9th century. The *San Francisco Convent* and the *Hospital San Juan de Dios* both date from the Renaissance.

Aquarium Puerto Banús

The picturesque marina in Marbella is also home to the marine observation centre Centro de Observación Marina, which aims to make the Mediterranean flora and fauna known to a wider public. Within the complex, which covers an area of 500 sq m, you can see virtually every kind of fish in the

Mediterranean, and also tropical fish. If you are brave enough, you may, as a newcomer to diving and accompanied by an instructor, go down to a depth of 3 metres in a special container, from which you can survey small sharks, lobsters and tuna fish at close quarters. You can even stroke and feed the rays as they glide past gracefully. *Daily 11 am–6 pm; admission 750 Ptas, reduced 550 Ptas*

Plaza de los Naranjos

★ The Square of the Orange Trees has a way of welcoming visitors into its familiar atmosphere. The octagonal *marble fountain* dates from the time of the Renaissance, the *Pilgrimage Chapel* from the 15th century, the *Town Hall* and the *Casa del Corregidor* (House of the provincial governor) from the 16th century. The interior of the Town Hall is decorated with particularly attractive frescoes and panelling.

Promenade La Alameda

The promenade is rich in tradition and is lined with centuries-old trees. The pines and rubber trees are especially attractive. You won't find more beautiful ceramic benches anywhere else on the coast.

RESTAURANTS

Los Bandidos

Popular restaurant, the food is international with a particular slant towards France. *Puerto Banús, Muelle Riviera M-35; Tel. 952 81 59 15; closed Sun; category 2*

California

❖ This fish restaurant, with its divine sea food, is certainly not short of clientele. Reservation essential in the evenings. *Av. Severo Ochoa 2; Tel. 952 86 34 66; closed Sun; category 2*

La Comedia
The right place for an intimate, romantic dinner on a tiny balcony. Appealing international cuisine. *Pl. de la Victoria; Tel. 952 77 64 78; closed lunch time and Mon; category 2*

La Pesquera Barbacoa
❖ Superb, simple fare right next to the beach. The speciality is peppers stuffed with cod. *Playa Alhambra del Mar; Tel. 952 77 04 64; daily; category 2–3*

Santiago
❖ Fish restaurant right next to the sea. *Boquerones fritos,* roast sardines, and *mero en salsa,* a juicy piece of sea bass in sauce, are the specialities. In the wine cellar 120,000 fine wines bide their time until they are uncorked. *Paseo Marítimo 5; Tel. 952 77 00 78; daily; category 1*

SHOPPING

Accessories
Fashion jewellery, handbags and leather accessories at *Princess Bea Auersperg (San Juan Bosco 6 and Puerto Banús, Paseo Benabola s/n).*

Men's shoes
The Spanish King has visited *Mocasines Pepe (Torre de Marbella, local 19),* at least 20 times and other members of the aristocracy are regular customers of the moccasin king of Andalusia. Even if you don't have blue blood in your veins, there is nothing to stop you from picking up a pair of shoes here, at prices starting from 25,000 Ptas.

Fashion
Something special for her at *Louis Féraud (Pl. Victoria)* or at *Luba,* a delightful boutique in *Puerto Banús (Muelle Ribera 17).* High-quality sportswear for him at low prices is to be had at *Bailey's (Pl. de Naranjos 1; open until midnight).* Cool designer models at *Elite (Puerto Banús, Paseo Benabola, Local 61 C).* Way-out beachware at reasonable prices at the *Boutique 007 (Puerto Banús, Muelle Ribera 4).*

ACCOMMODATION

Camping-Caravaning Marbella Playa
Situated between the sea and road, in the shade of leafy trees. Pool and warm showers. *N340 km 192.9; Tel. 952 83 39 98; Fax 952 83 39 99*

La Estrella
Little *hostal* on the coastal road. *15 rooms; C. San Cristóbal 36; Tel. 952 77 94 72; category 2–3*

Youth hostel (Albergue Juvenil de Marbella)
Youth hostel in the upper part of the town, 2 km away from the beach. Attractive reception area, pool in the park. 141 beds in 2- to 4-bed rooms. *Trapiche 2; Tel. 952 77 14 91; Fax 952 86 32 27*

Residencia Lima
Reasonably priced hotel in the town centre. No more than three minutes from the beach. *42 rooms; Av. Antonio Belón 2; Tel. 952 77 05 00; Fax 952 86 30 91; category 2–3*

Puente Romano
The hotel has almost acquired the status of a tourist attraction. The twenty-six three-storey buildings face up towards the sun and are

Golf freaks will find 162(!) such holes on the western Costa

surrounded by water jets and palm trees. The sub-tropical garden with more than 400 different kinds of plant, streams, waterfalls, hidden ponds and swimming pools is unusually beautiful. The furnishings are lavish, as befits an establishment classified as "One of the Leading Hotels of the World". *219 rooms; N 340 km 177; P. O. Box 204; Tel. 952 82 09 00; Fax 952 82 26 43; category 1*

SPORTS & EXCURSIONS

Ballooning

A particularly good time to set out on this venture is before sunrise. To add a touch of class, you can take champagne and tapas up into the air with you. Trips over Ronda and the indented coastline. *Aviación del Sol, March–Oct; Tel. 952 87 72 49; from 20,000 Ptas*

Golf

Take aim at a total of 162 holes in Marbella. Prices range from 3,500 to 20,000 Ptas. One of the finest is the 18-hole course *Golf Club Marbella (N 340 km 199; Tel. 952 83 05 00; open all year).*

Riding

The *Los Caireles Riding Club* is housed in the *Finca Los Almendros,* on the edge of the town. There are courses for beginners and daily excursions for experienced riders to nearby mountain villages. *Tues–Sun; Tel. 952 77 78 48*

Boat trips

You can both rent sailing and motor boats, and also receive instruction in sailing them, from *Club Náutico de Marbella (C. Padre José Vera; Tel. 952 77 43 76).* You can rent a yacht or take a trip on the high seas complete with skipper and crew *(Yacht Charters Marbella; Tel. 914 41 71 24).*

Tennis

Tenis El Casco (Urb. El Rosario; Tel. 952837651) is five minutes' drive from the town centre and has 6 clay courts and 4 hard courts.

ENTERTAINMENT

One of the nicest bars is *La Notte (Camino de la Cruz s/n, Las Lomas)*, a temple in Art Deco style for those who come alive at night and where celebrities rub shoulders and the piano plays until the early hours. The *Sinatra Bar (Puerto Banús, Muelle Ribera)*, at the harbour entrance of Puerto Banús is where the in-crowd comes and the music is loud. The tapa bar ✶ *Bodega La Venecia (Av. Miguel Cano 15)* has a pleasant atmosphere and attracts plenty of young customers. The most extravagent disco on the coast bears the name of its owner *Olivia Valère (Ctra. de Istán km 0.8)*, and is built in the style of a Moorish fortress. The drinks are expensive, but if you want the chance to share the dance floor with the royal familiy, you'll have to put up with this.

INFORMATION

Oficina de Turismo
Glorieta de la Fontanilla s/n (Paseo Marítimo); Tel. 952 77 14 42; Fax 952 77 94 57

SURROUNDING AREA

Ronda   **(111/E2)**
You can't fail to be moved by the barren landscape of the Serranía de Ronda where different visual effects occur depending on the position of the sun. Wild plants grow along the edge of the road also crossed by riders on donkeyback, and holm oaks, pines and Spanish fir trees form the backdrop. This was for many centuries the territory of the *bandoleros,* the bandits, who were the kings amongst the outlaws and whose exploits are today enshrined in myth. "As far as the eye can see, on all sides there is nothing other than a romantic theatrical backdrop", was Hemingway's impression of this place. Little, white villages peep out from behind rocky crests. Just before you reach Ronda there are so many of them that you could almost imagine that the mountains were covered in snow.

Ronda (pop. 34,000) itself, perched up on the rocks, is awesome in its beauty. The focal point of the town is the protected *Puente Nuevo* bridge over the El Tajo gorge, a 160-m-deep cleft in the rocky plateau, across which time and again throughout history enemies have faced each other and exchanged fire. It connects the historical centre of La Ciudad across the Rio Tajo with the new quarter of Mercadillo. It is a long time since Ronda last witnessed conflict. It has dropped into a slumber, lost in its own dreams – at least, when the last of the tourist buses have departed (avoid weekends and holidays!).

It is no surprise that the poet Rainer Maria Rilke was enthralled when he stayed in the town in 1912-13. It was in the *Hotel Reina Victoria (89 rooms; Av. Dr. Fleming 25; Tel. 952 87 12 40; Fax 952 87 10 75; category 1–2)* that he wrote the *Duino Elegies* and his room has been turned into a little museum that is open to visitors, with photos, drawings, books, Rilke's hotel bill, and even an almond twig on his writing desk. Today there is an Avenida named after the poet, a number of restaurants and bars also bear his name, and even one of the driving schools in the town insists on adorning each of its vehicles with his signature.

Its rich Muslim and Christian past have filled the town with many splendid buildings, palaces, churches and gateways. The *Puerta del Almocábar*, a Moorish town gate dating from the 13th century, takes you into the historical centre with its maze of alleys and the remains of baths built during the Arab epoch. The *Santa María la Mayor (daily 10 am–7 pm; admission 200 Ptas)* stands on a site a 13th century mosque. After the Reconquista, the attempt was made to remove all traces of Islam, but you can still make out remnants of the prayer chamber near the entrance. Photographers should not miss the *Palacio de Mondragón* with its *Local History Museum (Mon–Fri, 10 am–7 pm, Sat/Sun 10 am–3 pm; 250 Ptas)*, completed in 1314, later extended several times. The three inner courtyards, the garden and the view of the gorge are all attractive. However, the most beautiful feature is the path leading from the little, fenced-in square to the left of the palacio down the slope into the gorge. Stairs alternate with gravel as the path makes the descent of about 500 m. Don't forget that you will have to climb back up – but it will be worth it when you see that this is the best place to take photographs of the spectacular bridge.

The inhabitants of Ronda take the greatest pride in their *Plaza de Toros*, built in 1785 and as such the oldest bullfighting arena in Spain *(with bullfighting museum; daily 10 am–8 pm; 400 Ptas)*. This is where bullfighting first acquired the set of rules which are still in force today. Francisco Romero from Ronda was the first matador to come face to face with the bull on foot (previously they had done battle on horseback) waving the *muleta*, the red cloth. The first sentence in the rules state "A coward is no man". Romero's grandson Pedro is said to have fought until he was 80 and in that time to have killed more than 5,000 bulls without receiving so much as a scar.

Just opposite the arena, there is fare to match the occasion (e.g. bull's tail!) at *Pedro Romero (C. Virgen de la Paz 18; Tel. 952 87 11 10; daily; category 2–3)*, and also at � *Don Miguel (C. Villanueva 4; Tel. 952 87 10 90; daily; category 2-3)* with an unforgettable view from the terrace. If you wish to stay the night, a reasonably-priced option is the family guest house *Hostal Biarritz (C. Almendra 7; Tel. 952 87 29 10; category 3)*, or a more up-market choice is the ✲ *Parador de Ronda (78 rooms; Pl. de España; Tel. 952 87 75 00; Fax 952 87 81 88; category 1)*, where there is a view straight down into the gorge from your balcony. Information: *Oficina de Turismo; Pl. de España; Tel./Fax 952 87 12 72*

San Pedro de Alcántara (111/F3)

You will be surprised at how much further your money goes in this little town (pop. 20,000), 11 km from Marbella. Some distance from the town, at Río Verde, are the ruins of the *Roman settlement of Silniana*, which was destroyed in 356 AD by a seaquake.

Marina (106/A6, 111/F3)

At the most famous marina on the Mediterranean, and especially at the prestigious, picturesquely situated *Puerto Banús*, the most luxurious yachts of all still lie moored. *Cabo Pino*, 17 km further east, is the most modern.

Gorges, lakes and peaceful villages

These routes are marked in green on the map on the inside front cover and in the Road Atlas beginning on page 104

① UP COUNTRY FROM MALAGA AND MARBELLA

 The area upcountry from Almería kills three birds with one stone: white villages, an awe-inspiring gorge and a monument you can visit and even stay at. If you set out from Málaga and finish up in Castillo de Monda, this day tour covers approximately 150 km.

You leave *Málaga (S. 67)* on the N 357 in the direction of Cártama, the first few kilometres of which are built to highway standard. As you are leaving Campanilla you pick up the country road leading to Pizarra. Without warning, the city comes to an end and you find yourself out in the countryside. You now begin to see heavily burdened donkeys trotting along the dusty tracks beside the road, olive trees extending their gnarled boughs into the air, and at the time of year when they bloom, hundreds of hectares of sunflowers metamorphose into a yellow sea. Dried-out river beds full of gravel lie amongst the red, naked rocks. Nature dances to a completely different tune up here in the mountainous inland above the coast than it does be-side the sea. Fauna and flora of Europe and Africa are in evidence, lynxes and half-wild horses have survived in this unspoilt region, royal eagles brood and over a thousand species of migratory birds stop off here, flamingos and storks move solemnly through the barren, mountainous landscape.

To the right and left of you villages cling to the slopes, *pueblos blancos* with whitewashed walls. Let's hope you haven't forgotten your sunglasses to protect your eyes from the glare. The concentration of white has always been the best way of keeping the intense summer heat at bay. The Andalusians have the Moors to thank for this practice of reflecting rather than absorbing the rays of the sun. They were responsible for founding many a village in this region during their rule of almost 800 years. The North Africans were the first people to discover the inland, which they cherished as a refuge from the heat of the coast.

At Alora you take the road leading to Ardales, only to take an even smaller road almost immediately. You will soon come to the signposted *Garganta del Chorro,* an awe-inspiring gorge, through which the Río Guadalhorce rushes. Its rocky walls are as high as 400 m. The Málaga-Córdoba railway line runs through the mountain. On the mountain, the *Camino del Rey* (Path of the King) runs along the top of a steep precipice. Although it affords a thrilling view of the gorge, this adventure trip along such a narrow, mountainous path is only to be recommended for the most strong-willed – there are frequent rock falls, vertigo is almost guaranteed, and in places parts of the railing are missing. This is the place for those who want to feel the adrenaline running in their veins. Nobody is prevented from taking the Camino del Rey, and many people do this, although it is officially closed to tourists. The trip certainly has its own particular thrill and it is up to you to decide whether or not it is worth the risk. There is nobody to hold you back, but you should be certain that you are capable of retracing your steps if you find that you have bitten off more than you can chew.

You head in a northerly direction, and it only takes a few minutes to reach the local leisure area *Parque de Ardales*, the lake district of Andalusia. These lakes, fed by mountain springs, flash in emerald green among the overhanging pine woods. The three reservoirs centred around the town of Pantano del Chorro are little more than an hour by car from Málaga, but this is a totally different world with an alpine feel. Anglers perch on protruding rocks to dangle their lines out in the water, Spanish families picnic in the fine sand of the banks, pedal boats, kayaks and canoes fill the water,

which is clean and clear enough to make swimming there a delight. To the north of this artificially created lakeland is the largest natural lake in Andalusia, *Fuente de Piedra*. You can get here by taking the little road through the town of Estación de Bobadilla. The whole of the lake is a conservation area, and it is a must for ornithologists, as this is the only inland lake in Europe where flamingoes breed. You can stroll along the shore of the lake and observe these graceful animals in a natural setting. Whether you swim or take some kind of craft, it is forbidden to go near the bird island, which is heavily populated in spring. The presence of humans disturbs the birds and inhibits them from breeding. Even so, you will find that you should be able to get a few impressive snapshots from the shore.

Returning from Fuente de Piedra, first you drive along a stretch of the A 92 main road, then you take the N 382 as far as Campillos. From here, you turn into the winding country road 357, which twists and turns across the mountains as far as Cártama – a journey through an isolated, peaceful landscape. It doesn't take long to get to Coín along the N 355 from Cártama and now the traffic starts to get heavier. You bypass Coín and come into a fertile valley with orange and lemon groves, crowned by the town of *Monda*.

This is where two Englishmen acquired the *Castillo de Monda,* which according to the chronicles was destroyed by Saib Ibn Al Mundir in 990. This was a time of fierce military conflict between the Muslim royal houses for regional supremacy. And then, for more then 1,000 years it was the fate of the massive edifice above the town to remain in ruins. This state of affairs continued until the Englishmen, who had made their money from the shoe and video trades, began at the beginning of the 1990s to search for a property where they could rejoice in their homosexuality. Unfortunately, Spanish law prohibits the possession of historical monuments for purely private use. To get round this ban, the owners have created a hotel surrounding their own residential quarters.

An investment of nearly 3 million US$ was made, architects came from Málaga, craftsmen from Granada, artists from other regions of Spain. The building was fitted out tastefully and with an eye for detail. The walls are richly decorated with flowers, leaves and stars, and between them the name of Allah is emblazoned hundreds of times in white marble. There are suites in Moorish style, traditional ceiling beams in the restaurant, gleaming glass windows, intimate inner courtyards, peaceful nooks and crannies in the parapets where you can sit and contemplate, and water gurgling everywhere – right down to the bar. Following 1,000 years of stagnation, the Moorish age has come alive once more over Monda. Where once oriental potentates ruled, surrounded by the royal household and harem, today the guest stops off to relive this history first hand. If you want to stay, you can dine and relax like a pasha, but there is no longer a harem *(34 rooms; Tel. 952 45 71 42; Fax 952 45 73 36; category 1).*

The quickest way to get back to the coast is to go in a westward direction via Ojén to *Marbella (S. 86)* and Málaga.

② THE ATMOSPHERE AND BACKDROP OF THE WEST

The area upcountry from Almería is still unconquered by tourism. You will experience the reserved, quiet side of the region on this day tour covering about 250 km.

In physical terms, the distance from the mad hustle and bustle of *Almería (S. 53)* to Cabo de Gata is not much more than a stone's throw – but it feels like a journey from one continent to another. The *Sierra de Gata* is a little bit of Africa that has been transposed into Europe; it is the least hospitable part of the Iberian peninsula – a desert to the east of the almost sub-tropical, lush, fruitful stretch of land between Málaga and Almería. No other place in Europe has such low rainfall figures – about 150 mm per year. The sumptuous vegetation comes abruptly to an end, its place taken by a steppe landscape of agaves and cacti in the rain shadow of the mighty Sierra Nevada, which shimmers in the heat. Rugged cañons and dried-out river beds are its most striking features. The asphalt road, which is only well-built as far as the cape, passes one long, lonely, shadowless beach after another, paradises for individualists and naturists, particularly as the water, which is almost glaringly blue, is clear and home to a rich variety of sea life with many coral reefs. This is where the Costa del Sol merges into the Costa Blanca.

The captivating view across the Golfo de Almería alone is reason enough to make the journey into this region, totally unspoilt by tourism – its length of about 60 km makes it the longest stretch of the

Spanish coastline still in pristine condition. This view is all the more wonderful after dark, when the city harbour projects its reflection into the bay in the form of many thousands of tiny specks of light. The lighthouse stands on the steep, rocky coastline of the bay, at the point where the road snakes its way uphill. The *Mirador de las Sirenas* of the lighthouse affords a fantastic view out across bizarre cliff heads, where seals doze on rocks, flamingos make their way over salt deposits, cormorants emit powerful shrieks as they plunge greedily into the sea only to emerge again in the twinkling of an eye clutching their scaly, silvery prey. The almost complete absence of people means that the fauna is intact. There is nothing more than the odd finca and clutches of cactus. The peace and quiet comes as a unique and profound experience after days spent in the hurly-burly of the Costa del Sol.

From San José, you take a narrow, country road heading north to the Sierra de Alhamilla. Go in the direction of Níjar and then take road 370 towards *Tabernas*. There, in the middle of a terrain practically devoid of vegetation, stands a town consisting only of the wooden frames of houses and saloons. This ghost town is a curious leftover of the Italian Sergio Leone, who shot his "Italo" westerns here in deepest Spain. It has been named, appropriately, *Mini-Hollywood* and makes a great impression on the young *(daily 10 am–8 pm, winter until 7 pm; 1700 Ptas, children 750 Ptas; Ctra. de Murcia, km 138)*. The *Sierra de Alhamilla* is the only genuine desert in Europe – rugged, with no trees and virtually no plants. It is worth stopping now

and again, just to observe this moon landscape a little more closely, and also to breathe in the air, which is at its best a little off the road. It is dry and especially pure – it does your lungs the power of good. Astronomers also take advantage of the climatic conditions here. An observatory with the largest reflecting telescope in Europe is in operation on the 2,168-m-high *Calar Alto*. The *Observator* is open to visitors between 9 am–midday.

You continue on your way through the mountainous landscape along roads 92 and 348 fringing the south-eastern foothills of the Sierra Nevada. The road is narrow, the bends are sharp, the journey is lonely with hardly another car in sight – you couldn't wish for a starker contrast with the coast. At Alcolea you take the C 337 and shortly afterwards you come to *Berja*. This is where the heart of the wine connoisseur misses a beat. The town (pop. 11,000) is tucked into a valley the slopes of which are full of vines. This is one of the few places upcountry from the coast where you can watch without embarrassment the predominantly elderly residents in their twilight years. Everything is done slowly, following the rhythm of a past era, in accordance with eternal laws. There is nothing to be seen, apart from houses with windows, and balcony railings in the Arab tradition. One glance is enough to take in the remnants of the town walls and Arab wells. But don't miss the opportunity to stroll through the alleys and take in some of the atmosphere, to recharge your batteries in the peace and quiet, before you join the coastal highway to return to Almería.

Practical information

Important addresses and useful information for your visit to Granada and the Costa del Sol

AMERICAN & BRITISH ENGLISH

Marco Polo travel guides are written in British English. In North America certain terms and usages deviate from British usage. Some of the more frequently encountered examples are (American given first):
baggage = luggage; cab = taxi; car rental = car hire; drugstore = chemist; fall = autumn; first floor = ground floor; freeway/highway = motorway; gas(oline) = petrol; railroad = railway; restroom = toilet/lavatory; streetcar = tram; subway = underground/tube; toll-free numbers = freephone numbers; trailer = caravan; trunk = boot (of a car); vacation = holiday; wait staff = waiter/waitress; zip code = post code.

BANKS AND CREDIT CARDS

In general, opening hours are Mon–Fri 8.30 am–2 pm, Thurs until 6 pm. Spain has the densest network of ATMs anywhere in Europe. The usual credit cards are accepted at all high-class restaurants, in many hotels, large shops, at most filling stations and by car rental companies.

CAMPING

The number and quality of campsites on the Costa del Sol still leaves much to be desired, but a lot has been done in recent years. In particular, the sanitary facilities, the subject of much criticism in the past, have been improved. The average price for adults is 2,000, and for children 1,300 Ptas, whilst 2,000 Ptas is charged for a car, tent or caravan. Unauthorised camping is frowned on, and can be downright dangerous in dried-out river beds.

CAR RENTAL

The international car rental firms are represented at all airports, in cities and major towns. The rent of a car will cost, according to the type, 4,000– 10,000 Ptas per day, plus a kilometre charge and an extra charge for fully comprehensive insurance. Some travel organisations offer fly & drive packages at particularly attractive prices. Cars are only rented to drivers aged over 21 who have been in possession of a driving licence for at least one year. The vehicles are not always in optimal condition – as a rule of thumb, those cars on offer at the cheapest prices are the least well-maintained.

CUSTOMS

There are no more customs restrictions for private travellers within the EU. The following items may be imported by passengers from countries outside the EU: 200 cigarettes, gifts up to the value of app. 6,200 Ptas.

DRIVING

Speed limits: in built-up areas: 50 km/h; on secondary roads: 90 km/h; on highways: 120 km/h. The legal limit is 50 mg alcohol/100 ml of blood. It is recommended you bring a green insurance card with you and take out international travel insurance and fully comprehensive insurance policies. There is a good network of filling stations selling lead-free gas *(sin plomo)*. In the event of an accident, make sure you have two (preferably Spanish) witnesses, and notify your own third party insurer and its Spanish agency. Do not sign any admission of guilt! In the case of minor accidents, come to an agreement with the other party, who is likely to be under-insured – it saves a lot of trouble later. If major damage occurs, or if someone is injured, you must notify the police. Cars can be rented for around 9,200 Ptas per day (small models).

EMBASSIES & CONSULATES

British Embassy
Calle de Fernando el Santo 16, 28010 Madrid; Tel. (91) 700 8200; Fax (91) 700 8272

British Consulate General
Marques de la Ensenada 16, 2nd Floor, Centro Colon, 28004 Madrid. (Other consulates in Barcelona, Málaga, etc.)

Embassy of the United States of America
Serrano 75, 28006 Madrid; Tel. (91) 587 2200; Fax (91) 587 2303; Web site: http://www.embusa.es

Canadian Embassy
Edificio Goya, Calle Nunez de Balboa 35, 28001 Madrid; Tel. (91) 423 3250; Fax (91) 423 3251; Web site: http://www.canada-es.org (Consulates in Barcelona and Málaga)

EMERGENCIES

General 112, Police *(policía)* 091, Ambulance *(ambulancia)* 061

FISHING

In the area upcountry from the Costa del Sol and in the province of Granada there are rivers and reservoirs rich in fish. A fishing permit is required. This is obtainable from the provincial directorate of the conservation authority Icona.

GOLF

The 85-kilometre stretch of the N 340 between Málaga and San Roque on the Costa del Sol

Man had to dissapear from the roadsides. The cunning Spanish declared the bull to be a "national cultural property". With the result that the toro was allowed

has the highest concentration of golf courses in the world – 32 courses. There are a total of 46 courses in the area covered by this guide. Information: *www.golfpoint.com*

HEALTH

Citizens from EU countries who are covered by health insurance schemes in their own countries are also covered in Spain. If you take form E111 along with you, it will make matters easier. Non-EU visitors are advised to take out additional medical insurance before departure. Medical treatment in Granada and on the Costa del Sol is good, in the rural areas up-country treatment is provided by local accident stations *(casa de socorro)*. Pharmacies *(farmacia)* are marked with a green cross.

HOTELS

As a rule, prices are reasonable. Hotels in the luxury class have prices to match. Whatever the establishment, the rule is that the prices

must be displayed on the door to the room. Complaints should be addressed to the local tourist authorities. The *paradores* have a charm of their own – these are historical buildings (old hunting lodges, monasteries, palaces) that have been converted into hotels and they are often in unusual locations. Seven of these are mentioned in the guide. They are often cheaper than ordinary hotels of a similar standard. If you are looking for reasonably priced holiday rooms and flats, apply to *RAAR (Red Andaluza de Alojamientos Rurales), Apartado de Correos 2035, E-04080 Almería; Tel. 0034/950 26 50 18; Fax 950 27 04 31, www.raar.es.*

INFORMATION

Internet
www.andalucia.org; www.tourspain.es

Spanish Tourist Office:

In the UK:
Spanish National Tourist Office 22–23 Manchester Square,

London W1M 5AP
Tel. (020) 7486 8077 or (0900)
166 9920; Fax (020) 7486 8034
Web site: http://www.tourspain.es

In the USA:

Spanish Tourist Office
666 Fifth Avenue, 35th Floor
New York, NY 10103
Tel. (212) 2658822 or (1 888)
657 7246 (toll free, USA only)
Fax (212) 265 8864
E-mail: oetny@tourspain.es
Web site: http://www.okspain.org

In Canada:

Spanish Tourist Office
2 Bloor Street West, 34th Floor,
Suite 3402
Toronto, Ontario M4W 3E2
Tel. (416) 961 3131
Fax (416) 961 1992
E-mail: toronto@tourspain.es
Web site:
http://www.tourspain.toronto.on.ca

MEASURES & WEIGHTS

1 cm	0.39 inches
1 m	1.09 yards
	(3.28 feet)
1 km	0.62 miles
1 m²	1.20 sq. yards
1 ha	2.47 acres
1 km²	0.39 sq. miles
1 g	0.035 ounces
1 kg	2.21 pounds
1 British ton	1016 kg
1 US ton	907 kg

1 litre is equivalent to 0.22 Imperial
gallons and 0.26 US gallons

NEWSPAPERS

All leading international newspapers and magazines are available in the larger, and even smaller, towns, although often with a delay of one day.

NUDITY

To walk around anywhere topless is not a problem, but complete nudity is not tolerated on public beaches.

OPENING HOURS

The vast majority of shops open from 9.30 am–2 pm and from 5 pm–8 or 8.30 pm, on Sat often only in the mornings. These times are by no means cast in stone, and especially in the tourist centres supermarkets often stay open all day and at weekends. Petrol stations in central locations do not observe the siesta, in other places it is the rule.

PASSPORT & VISA

There are no longer passport formalities for visitors from any of the EU countries; nevertheless you should take your passport or identity card in case it should be required. Citizens of non-EU countries need a passport. No visas are required by American and Canadian citizens. Children under 16 need their own identity card or an entry in the passport of their parents.

PETS

Pets must have been inoculated against rabies at least 30 days before entry, and evidence of this is required in the form of a vaccination certificate. A certificate, issued by a veterinarian and certified by a Spanish consulate, stating that the animal is in good health is also required.

POST

Post offices are open on Mon–Fri from 8 am–8 pm, on Sat until 2 pm. You can also get stamps from tobacco shops and in many hotels.

PUBLIC TRANSPORT

Wherever there is a fairly frequent service, public transport is often a good way of getting about in the South of Spain, with its serious traffic congestion. There are frequent bus services in towns and cities, and also to all major tourist attractions outside the towns. In the central Costa del Sol, the suburban railway between Málaga and Fuengirola is to be recommended.

RIDING

Riding has a very long history in this part of the world – cave drawings attest to its existence 10,000 years ago. Andalusia is horse-breeding territory and, not surprisingly, riding is one of the great tourist attractions. The following riding establishments can be recommended: *Escuela de Arte Ecuestre Costa del Sol, Estepona; Tel. 952 80 52 60; Fax 952 80 49 53; Centro de Equitación Club El Ranchito, C. Sendal del Pilar 4, Torremolinos; Tel. 952 38 30 63; Club Hípico de Benalmádena, Finca Los Caballeros, Urb. Torrequebrada Norte, Benalmádena; Tel. 952 56 84 84, Fax 952 56 82 00*

STAYING IN PARKS

The largest specialist in Andalusia for accommodation in isolated villages in nature parks is *Rural-Andalus (29007 Málaga, C. Don Cristián 10; Tel. 952 27 62 29; Fax 952 27 65 56)*. The houses are old, but without exception well-renovated and are let at prices ranging from 35,000 –58,000 Ptas per week. This is a great news for families, nature lovers and all those who yearn to get away from the rat race for a week or two.

TELEPHONE

Public telephones operate on *tarjeta de teléfono* priced at 1,000 or 2,000 Ptas, obtainable from tobacco shops. To call another country from Spain you dial 00 and then the appropriate country code (UK 44, for the USA and Canada 1, for Ireland 353), followed by the area code without the 0. The dialing code for Spain is 0034. Within Spain, there are no dialing codes; these have now been incorporated into the subscriber numbers. For this reason, you must dial the initial 9 when you call from abroad.

WHEN TO GO

Any time of the year is a good time to visit the Costa del Sol – in winter the temperatures are still generally pleasantly warm. Even December has an average of five hours of sunshine per day, and some hardened souls greet the arrival of the New Year with a dip in the sea, at a temperature of some 16°C (61°F). The main season lasts from the end of April to mid-October, and prices everywhere are bumped up during this period. Winters in Granada and the inlying areas are a lot colder, although it is rare to see temperatures below zero – with the exception of Sierra Nevada, where snow is guaranteed from December to April. In the middle of summer, temperatures can exceed 40°C (104°F) on some days.

YOUTH HOSTELS

Remeber that not all youth hostels are open all year long. The cost of staying a night generally ranges between 1,400 and 2,500 Ptas. The Spanish Youth Hostel Association is known as the *Red Española de Albergues Juveniles, 28006 Madrid, C. Ortega y Gasset 71; Tel. 913 47 77 00.*

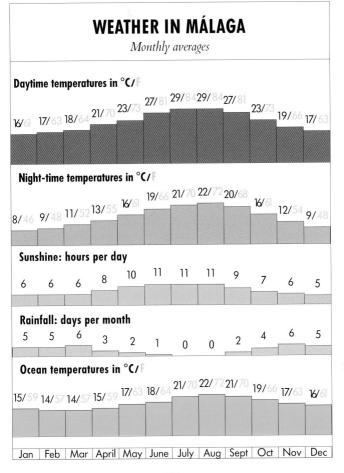

WEATHER IN MÁLAGA
Monthly averages

Daytime temperatures in °C/F

16/61 17/63 18/64 21/70 23/73 27/81 29/84 29/84 27/81 23/73 19/66 17/63

Night-time temperatures in °C/F

8/46 9/48 11/52 13/55 16/61 19/66 21/70 22/72 20/68 16/61 12/54 9/48

Sunshine: hours per day

6 6 6 8 10 11 11 11 9 7 6 5

Rainfall: days per month

5 5 6 3 2 1 0 0 2 4 6 5

Ocean temperatures in °C/F

15/59 14/57 14/57 15/59 17/63 18/64 21/70 22/72 21/70 19/66 17/63 16/61

| Jan | Feb | Mar | April | May | June | July | Aug | Sept | Oct | Nov | Dec |

Do's and don'ts

How to avoid some of the traps and pitfalls that face the unwary traveller at the Costa del Sol

Drugs

The Calderería Nueva with its pubs and tea bars is the most attractive stairway alley in Granada. This is also where drug dealers, predominantly of North African origin, operate. These guys can be awfully persistent and you would be well advised to make it very clear that you are not interested, as the penalties for drug possession and dealing are very severe. You should certainly not get mixed up in this business in any way at all.

Passing through the Barrio de la Chanca in Almería

The romantic ascent to the Alcazaba through the gypsy quarter La Chanca which is on the seaward side, is not advisable if you are on your own or, particularly, after dark. These people, living in their poverty-filled slums, are not interested in tourists and certainly do not wish to be photographed in their "picturesque" poverty. It is better to take the signposted route from the Calle Almanzor close to the Plaza Vieja.

Postcards which are not posted

Shops and traders make a habit of selling postcards and stamps and invite you to leave them with the seller once you have written them out, with the promise that they will be posted. You should be aware that this promise may lack sincerity. Only the better hotels are authorised to send out postcards.

Self-styled parking attendants

Poverty and unemployment make people inventive. Young men in particular are known to create their own jobs as "parking attendants", who offer to watch over parked cars or to guide a car into one of the cramped parking spaces. "Veinte duros, por favor" ("Hundred pesetas, please"), they then demand as a payment for their imposed service. The best thing to do is pay up, otherwise this self-styled protector of other people's property will most likely be the one who breaks into your car.

Unprotected sexual contact

More people in Spain die of AIDS than in traffic accidents. The country is number one in the European AIDS league table. The wide distribution of the disease is attributed to the high number of HIV-infected drug addicts. The next most important factor, according to the statistics, is the number of heterosexuals, especially men aged between 25–40, who have unprotected sex with different partners.

Road Atlas of the Costa del Sol

*Please refer to back cover for an overview
of this Road Atlas*

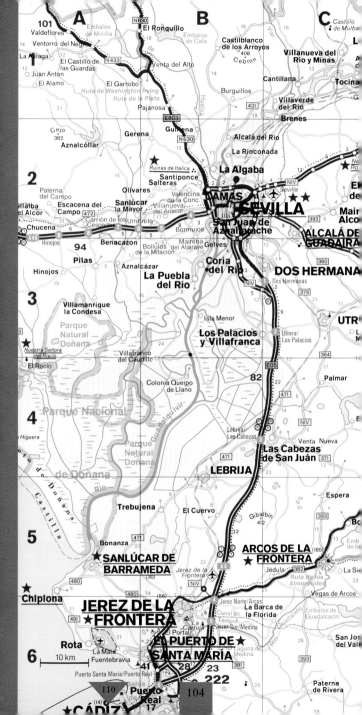

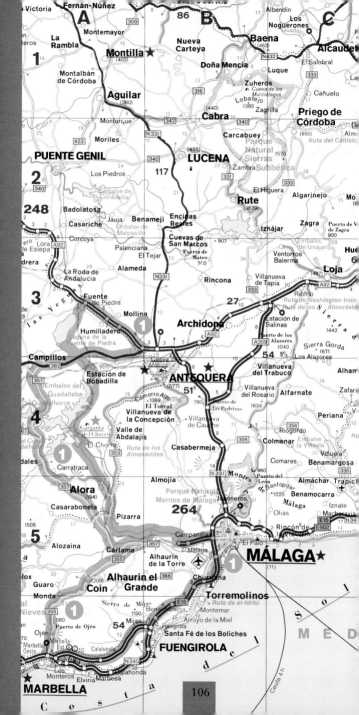

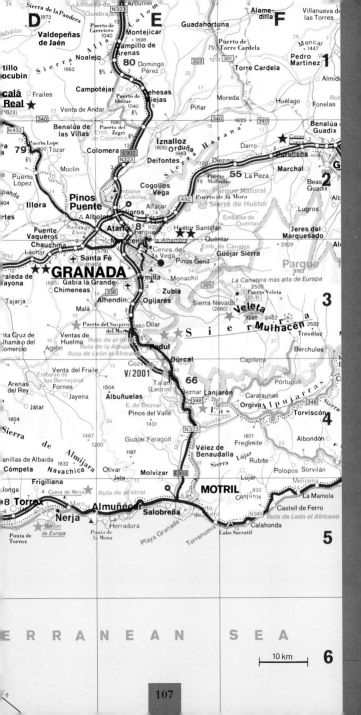

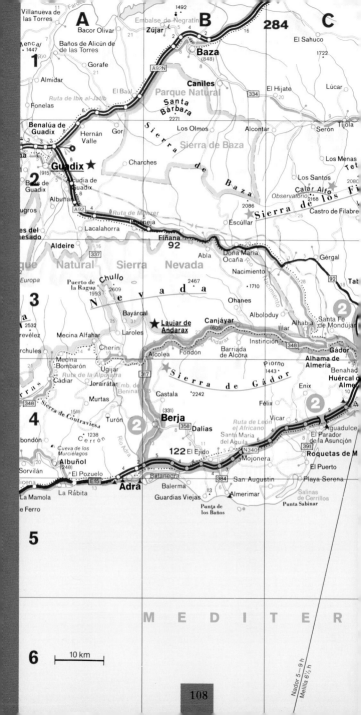

A

B

C

1

Villanueva de las Torres

Bacor Olivar

Zújar

Embalse de Negratín

El Sahuco

284

Baños de Alicún de las Torres

Baza
(848)

Gorafe

Mencal
1447

Río

Almidar

A92N

Caniles

El Hijate

Lúcar

Fonelas

Ruta de Ibn al-Jatib

El Baúl

Parque Natural

Santa
Bárbara
2271

Los Olmos

334

Serón

Tíjola

Benalúa de Guadix

Gor

Sierra de Baza

Alcontar

Los Menas

Hernán Valle

S i e r r a

Tet

Guadix ★

Charches

Sierra de Baza

Los Santos

2

(915)

Baños de Guadix

Acudia de Guadix

Albuñán

d e

B a z a

Los Santos

Observatorio
2168

Calar Alto
2168

208C

2086

Sierra de los Fi

ugros

A92

Ruta de Muñzer

Castro de Filabre

es del tesado

Lacalahorra

Aldeire

337

Finaña
92

Escúllar

26

Parque

Natural

Sierra

Nevada

Abla

Doña María Ocaña

Río

Gérgal

92

Tat

Europa

Puerto de la Ragua
1993

Chullo
2609

2467

Nacimiento

2

N e v a d a

Ohanes

1710

a

2532

revélez

Bayárcal

Alboloduy

Alhabia

Santa Fe de Mondújar

rchules

Mecina Alfahar

25

31

Laroles

Canjáyar
(605)

Illar

348

3

Cherín

★ Laujar de Andarax

Andarax

Instinción

Gádor

Mecina Bombarón

Ugíjar

Alcolea

Fondón

Barriada de Alcora

Alhama de Almería

Cádiar

Ruta de la Alpujarra

Joraírátar

Piorno
1443

Benahad

Huércal
Alme

Murtas

Emb. de Benín

S i e r r a   d e   G á d o r

Enix

348

Castala

2242

Félix

2

Sierra de Contraviesa

Turón

1511

Berja

331

Vícar

Aguadulce

4

bondón

Cerrón
1238

358

Dalías

Ruta de León el Africano

El Parador de la Asunción

391

Cueva de los Murciélagos

Albuñol
(248)

Río Adra

122 El Ejido

Santa María del Águila

N340

Mojonera

Roquetas de M

Sorvilán

El Pozuelo

Balanegra

El Puerto

icena

La Rábita

Adra

Balerma

384

San Augustín

Playa Serena

La Mamola

13

Guardias Viejas

Almerimar

Salinas de Cerrillos

e Ferro

Punta de los Baños

Punta Sabinar

5

M   E   D   I   T   E   R

6

| 10 km

Nador 5 – 9 h

Melilla 6½ h

108

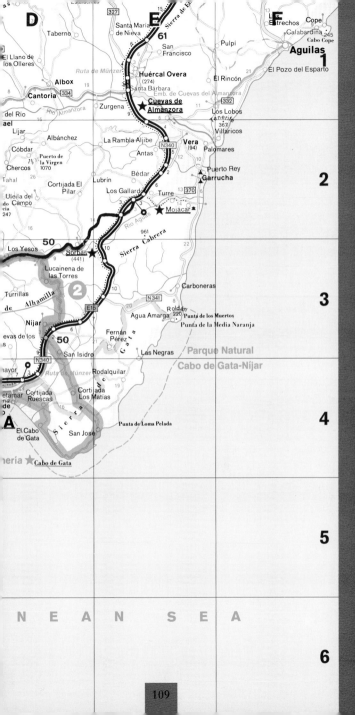

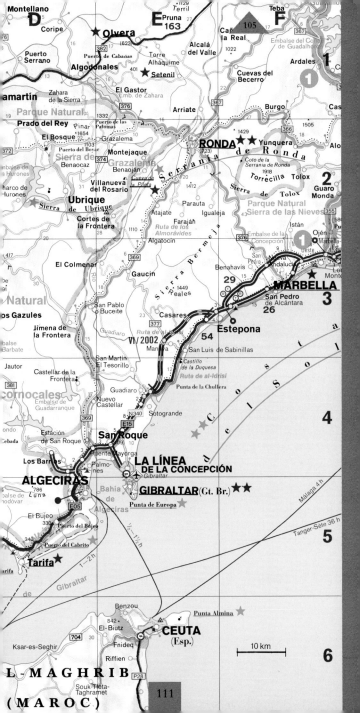

ROAD ATLAS LEGEND

le Mans-Est Autobahn mit Anschlussstelle
Motorway with junction

Datum, Date Autobahn in Bau
Motorway under construction

Datum, Date Autobahn in Planung
Motorway projected

ℝ Raststätte mit
Übernachtungsmöglichkeit
Roadside restaurant and hotel

ⓡ Raststätte ohne
Übernachtungsmöglichkeit
Roadside restaurant

ⓘ Erfrischungsstelle, Kiosk
Snackbar, kiosk

ⓣ Tankstelle
Filling-station

Autobahnähnliche Schnell-
straße mit Anschlussstelle
Dual carriage-way with
motorway characteristics
with junction

Straße mit zwei
getrennten Fahrbahnen
Dual carriage-way

Durchgangsstraße
Thoroughfare

Wichtige Hauptstraße
Important main road

Hauptstraße
Main road

Sonstige Straße
Other road

Fernverkehrsbahn
Main line railway

Bergbahn
Mountain railway

Autotransport
per Bahn
Transport of cars
by railway

Autofähre
Car ferry

Schifffahrtslinie
Shipping route

Landschaftlich besonders
schöne Strecke
Route with
beautiful scenery

*Routes
des Crêtes* Touristenstraße
Tourist route

Straße gegen Gebühr befahrbar
Toll road

X — X — X Straße für Kraftfahrzeuge
gesperrt
Road closed
to motor traffic

Zeitlich geregelter Verkehr
Temporal regulated traffic

◄— ◄ 15% Bedeutende Steigungen
Important gradients

Kultur
Culture

★★ **PARIS**
★★ *la Alhambra* Eine Reise wert
Worth a journey

★ **TRENTO**
★ *Comburg* Lohnt einen Umweg
Worth a detour

Landschaft
Landscape

★★ **Rodos**
★★ *Fingal's cave* Eine Reise wert
Worth a journey

★ **Korab**
★ *Jaskinia raj* Lohnt einen Umweg
Worth a detour

☀ ↯ Besonders schöner Ausblick
Important panoramic view

Nationalpark, Naturpark
National park, nature park

Sperrgebiet
Prohibited area

4807 ▲ Bergspitze mit Höhenangabe
in Metern
Mountain summit with height
in metres

(630) Ortshöhe
Elevation

♦ Kirche
Church

♦ Kirchenruine
Church ruin

♦ Kloster
Monastery

♦ Klosterruine
Monastery ruin

♦ Schloss, Burg
Palace, castle

♦ Schloss-, Burgruine
Palace ruin, castle ruin

♦ Denkmal
Monument

╱ Wasserfall
Waterfall

⌒ Höhle
Cave

∴ Ruinenstätte
Ruins

· Sonstiges Objekt
Other object

△ Jugendherberge
Youth hostel

🏖 🏄 Badestrand · Surfen
Bathing beach · Surfing

🤿 🎣 Tauchen · Fischen
Diving · Fishing

✈ Verkehrsflughafen
Airport

⊕ ⊕ Regionalflughafen · Flugplatz
Regional airport · Airfield

10 km

INDEX

This index lists all the main places, popular destinations, as well as all sights and museums in Granada and Málaga mentioned in this guide. Numbers in bold indicate a main entry, italics a photograph.

What do you get for your money?

Notes are in denominations of 1,000, 2,000, 5,000 and 10,000 Ptas and coins are in denominations of 1, 5, 25, 50, 100, 200 and 500.

Breakfast will set you back 300–600 Ptas, and you should expect to pay at least 3,000 Ptas for lunch or dinner. A mineral water costs 100 Ptas., and a glass of orange juice, beer or wine costs 150–175 Ptas. Tapas start from 150 Ptas. You may be able to find a room in an upcountry hotel for well under 8,600 Ptas. On the other hand, if you are thinking about luxury establishments on the coast, you are talking about prices above 43,000 Ptas, although this area also has plenty of accommodation to suit more restricted budgets. As everywhere, the rule is to compare prices. Marbella, for example, is on average one third cheaper than Torremolinos, although there is no great difference in quality between the two places.

There is a great abundance of ATMs, where you can use your bank card to withdraw cash. MasterCard, American Express, Diners Club and Visa are accepted almost everywhere, even at petrol stations. International travellers cheques and Eurocheques are are also widely accepted. Although you can usually get a better exchange rate in Spain than you can at home.

Ptas	£	US$	Can$
100	0.35	0.51	0.78
250	0.88	1.28	1.94
500	1.77	2.56	3.88
750	2.65	3.84	5.83
1,000	3.53	5.11	7.69
1,500	5.30	7.67	11.65
2,000	7.07	10.23	15.54
3,000	10.60	15.34	23.30
4,000	14.14	20.46	31.07
5,000	17.67	25.57	38.84
6,000	21.20	30.69	46.61
7,500	26.50	38.36	58.26
10,000	35.34	51.15	77.68
12,500	44.17	63.93	97.10
15,000	53.01	76.72	116.52
25,000	88.35	127.87	194.20
40,000	141.36	204.59	310.72
50,000	176.70	255.73	388.40
60,000	212.04	306.88	466.08
75,000	265.05	383.60	582.60
100,000	353.40	511.46	776.81

How to say it – communication made easy!